The
American War Congress
and Zionism

Statements by Members of the
American War Congress
on the
Jewish National Movement

ZIONIST ORGANIZATION OF AMERICA
55 FIFTH AVENUE, NEW YORK
1919

The Zionist Organization of America gratefully acknowledges its indebtedness to Mr. Reuben Fink, of Washington, for his services in the compilation of this material.

———

February, 1919

Introductory Note

In 1897, after seventeen centuries of exile, the Jewish people, through an International Congress assembled at Basle, Switzerland, formulated its demand for a "publicly secured and legally assured homeland in Palestine." In 1917, only twenty years later, Great Britain indorsed the Jewish position and pledged, upon her strength and her prestige, the realization of the Basle Platform. Thus, this project, from its inception, by a people which, however prodigal of effort and sacrifice, nevertheless lacked the political and military power to effect its design, has developed into one of the war aims of the nation possessing the best equipment, political and military, to secure these terms of peace to which it is committed.

The Declaration to support the Jewish National enterprise followed the military penetration of Palestine during the successful campaign inaugurated by Great Britain in the late summer and the autumn of 1917. This pledge was published on behalf of the British Government by the Honorable Arthur J. Balfour, Secretary of State for Foreign Affairs, in his letter to Lord Rothschild, on November second of that year. Since that time, Great Britain has proceeded with the consummation of her purpose by effecting the complete military occupation of Palestine and by the installation of the Zionist Commission, which administers, under British protection, the affairs of Jewish Palestine.

The Zionist Organization of America, in order to ascertain the sentiment of the members of the Legislature towards the British Declaration particularly, and towards the Zionist movement in general, and to inform itself of what action, executive or legislative, the War-Congress would be inclined to recommend or approve, sent to each member of both Houses, on June 11, 1918, a copy of the following letter:

5

"On November 2, 1917, the British Government, through the Honorable Arthur J. Balfour, Secretary of State for Foreign Affairs, officially declared its sympathy with Zionist aspirations, saying:

'His Majesty's Government view with favor the establishment in Palestine of a National Home for the Jewish people, and will use their best endeavours to facilitate the achievement of this object, it being clearly understood that nothing shall be done which may prejudice the civil and religious rights of non-Jewish communities in Palestine, or the rights and political status enjoyed by Jews in any other country.'

"This declaration was officially indorsed by the French Government on February 11, 1918, and again by the Italian Government on February 23, 1918.

"In view of President Wilson's utterances in favor of the rights of all similar nationalities, which are to be given the opportunity of determining their own futures, it is of the utmost interest to the Jewish people of the United States to be informed of the opinion of the members of the United States Senate and of the House of Representatives on this important question.

"We, therefore, take the liberty of addressing you at this time with the following inquiries:

"1. Do you approve the official Declaration of England, France and Italy on the Zionist question, as quoted above?

"2. Would you please let us have your reasons for favoring the Declaration? (If you do *not* favor it, please give us your reasons.)

"3. Do you favor action by the United States Government in line with the British Declaration, now or within the near future?

"4. Do you favor the adoption of an appropriate resolution by Congress in favor of the establishment in Palestine of a Jewish National Centre?

"5. What are your views in general with regard to the effort of the Jewish people to establish a national home in Palestine?"

In addition to the letters received by the Zionist Organization from the members of the War Congress, this book contains the statements of the governments pledged to support the Jewish national aspirations.

Besides Great Britain, Italy and France, the governments of Serbia, Holland, Greece, Siam, China and Japan have through official pronouncements committed themselves to the support of the project to establish a Jewish Homeland in Palestine. Whereas no action in line with the British Declaration has been taken by the Government of the United States, President Wilson in his letter to Rabbi Wise, on the thirty-first of August, 1918, expressed his sincere interest in the work of reconstruction in Palestine, and his satisfaction over the growth of the Zionist movement in the Allied countries and in the United States.

The fact that the statements of the members of Congress were received as early as June and as recently as December, 1918, will explain why some of them only have been written in the light of the President's letter.

The Balfour Declaration

Letter to Lord Rothschild from Mr. Arthur James Balfour, Secretary of State for Foreign Affairs:

Foreign Office, Nov. 2nd, 1917.

Dear Lord Rothschild:

I have much pleasure in conveying to you on behalf of His Majesty's Government, the following declaration of sympathy with Jewish Zionist aspirations, which has been submitted to, and approved by, the Cabinet:

"His Majesty's Government view with favor the establishment in Palestine of a National Home for the Jewish people, and will use their best endeavours to facilitate the achievement of this object, it being clearly understood that nothing shall be done which may prejudice the civil and religious rights and political status enjoyed by Jews in any other country."

I should be grateful if you would bring this declaration to the knowledge of the Zionist Federation.

Yours sincerely,

ARTHUR JAMES BALFOUR.

8

Letter of President Wilson to Rabbi Stephen S. Wise

The White House, Washington, 31 August, 1918.

My Dear Rabbi Wise:

I have watched with deep and sincere interest the reconstructive work which the Weizmann Commission has done in Palestine at the instance of the British Government, and I welcome an opportunity to express the satisfaction I have felt in the progress of the Zionist movement in the United States and in the Allied countries since the declaration by Mr. Balfour on behalf of the British Government, of Great Britain's approval of the establishment in Palestine of a national home for the Jewish people, and his promise that the British Government would use its best endeavors to facilitate the achievement of that object, with the understanding that nothing would be done to prejudice the civil and religious rights of non-Jewish people in Palestine or the rights and political status enjoyed by Jews in other countries.

I think that all Americans will be deeply moved by the report that even in this time of stress the Weizmann Commission has been able to lay the foundation of the Hebrew University at Jerusalem, with the promise that that bears of spiritual rebirth.

Cordially and sincerely yours,

WOODROW WILSON.

Dr. Stephen S. Wise, Chairman, Provisional Executive Committee for General Zionist Affairs, New York.

9

Government Indorsements

of Jewish National Aspirations and of the British Declaration

SERBIA

The following letter, of December 27, 1917, from Milenko Vesnitch, the head of the recent Serbian Mission to the United States, was sent to Capt. David Albala, a veteran of the Serbian Army, and forwarded by him to the Provisional Zionist Committee:

Serbian War Mission to the United States.

Dear Captain Albala:

I wish you to express to your Jewish brothers the sympathy of our Government and of our people for the just endeavor of resuscitating their beloved country in Palestine which will enable them to take their place in the future Society of Nations according to their numerous capacities and to their unquestioned right. We are sure that this will not only be to their own interest, but at the same time to that of the whole of humanity.

You know, dear Captain Albala, that there is no other nation in the world sympathizing with this plan more than Serbia. Do we not shed bitter tears on the rivers of Babylon in sight of our beloved land, lost only a short time ago? How should we not participate in your clamors and sorrows lasting ages and generations, especially when our countrymen of your origin and religion have fought for their Serbian fatherland as well as the best of our soldiers.

It will be a sad thing for us to see any of our Jewish fellow-citizens leaving us to return to their promised land, but we shall console ourselves in the hope that they will stand as brothers and leave with us a good part of their hearts and that they will be the strongest tie between free Israel and Serbia.

Believe me, dear Captain Albala,

Very sincerely yours,

VESNITCH.

FRANCE

The French Government made the following official declaration in favor of a Jewish State in Palestine in accord with the Declaration to the same effect, made by the British Cabinet on November 2, 1917.

The Provisional Executive Committee for General Zionist Affairs has been authorized by M. Tardieu, the French High Commissioner to the United States, to make public the following communications bearing on this subject:

Message from Foreign Minister Pichon to M. Tardieu:

Feb. 12, 1918.

Having seen M. Sokolow (representative of the Zionist Organizations), I authorized him to state that, as regards the question, our views were essentially the same as the views entertained by the British Government.

(Naval Radio, from the Press Bureau of The Ministry of Foreign Affairs)

M. Sokolow was received today by M. Stephen Pichon. M. Pichon was happy to reaffirm that the understanding is complete between the French and the British Governments, concerning the question of the Jewish establishment in Palestine.

ITALY

Through its Ambassador at the Court of St. James, the Italian Government, on Feb. 25, 1918, officially signified its approval of the English and French Declarations in favor of the Zionist movement and of a Jewish National Homeland in Palestine. Mr. Nahum Sokolow, representative in London of the Zionist International Political Committee, received from Ambassador Imperiali, the following formal statement of Italy's attitude of these questions:

"On the instructions of His Excellency, Baron Sonnino, His Majesty's Minister for Foreign Affairs, I have the honour to inform you that H. M. Government is pleased to confirm the declarations already made through their representatives in Washington, the Hague and Salonica, to the effect that they will use their best endeavours to facilitate the establishment in

11

Palestine of a Jewish National Centre, it being understood that this shall not prejudice the legal or political status enjoyed by Jews in any other country."

GREECE

On March 14th, 1918, M. Politis, the Greek Minister for Foreign Affairs, stated in the Chamber of Deputies:

"I have already had occasion in Salonika to express the very sincere sympathy of the Liberal party and of all Hellenes for the Jewish Nation, for twenty centuries the victim of misunderstandings and persecutions. I am glad to renew today the promise which I then gave that at the right moment the Liberal Government will put forth every effort to assist the national task of the Jews in full accord with the great Allies of Greece. Apart from the motives of sympathy which we have had for the Jewish race, a new bond is now added. Among other points in common, the Jewish race and the Greek race have that of both belonging with those races which have ceased to be subjected to persecution. At this moment when Hellenism has been literally led to exhaustion by the barbarians of the East, I address with emotion to the Jewish race all my wishes for their establishment as a nation."

HOLLAND

Mr. Jacobus Kann, President of the Dutch Zionist Federation, was authorized by the Dutch Government to declare that it is sympathetic toward Zionist aspirations.

SIAM

The Zionist Organization of America received the text of a statement issued by the Siamese Government expressing its approval of the plan to establish in Palestine a National Homeland for the Jewish people. The statement was issued to Mr. E. S. Kadoorie, one of the leading bankers of China and President of the Shanghai Zionist Association, by H. R. H. Prince Devawongse Varopakar, Siamese Minister for Foreign Affairs. It reads as follows:

Foreign Office, Bangkok, August 22, 1918.

Dear Sir:

I have the honour to state that the Royal Siamese Government expresses its accord with the sympathetic position taken by its Allies with reference to the establishment of Palestine as a National Home for the Jewish people and, in co-operation with the Allied Powers, will use its best endeavours to facilitate the achievement of this object, it being clearly understood that nothing will be done that may prejudice the civil or religious rights of existing non-Jewish communities in Palestine.

I am, very truly yours,

DEVAWONGSE.

CHINA

The Zionist Organization of America received a cablegram from Mr. E. S. Kadoorie, President, and N. E. B. Ezra, Secretary of the Shanghai Zionist Association, informing it that on Dec. 14, 1918, the Chinese Government had officially endorsed the project for establishing a Jewish Homeland in Palestine. The text of the Chinese endorsement is as follows:

The Chinese Government expresses its complete accord with Great Britain's proposals for the restoration of Palestine as the National Home of the Jewish people, it being clearly understood that nothing shall be done which may prejudice the civil and religious rights of existing non-Jewish communities in Palestine or the rights and political status enjoyed by Jews in any other country, and will co-operate with her Allies at the Peace Conference in the attaining of that object.

JAPAN

The government of Japan authorized its Ambassador to Great Britain to announce its approval of the project to establish in Palestine a Jewish National Homeland in accordance with the principles enunciated in the Balfour Declaration of November 2, 1917.

Members of Congress
From Whom Statements Have Been Received
SENATORS

ALABAMA
John H. Bankhead

ARIZONA
Marcus A. Smith

ARKANSAS
William F. Kirby
Joseph T. Robinson

CALIFORNIA
James D. Phelan

COLORADO
Charles S. Thomas

CONNECTICUT
George P. McLean

DELAWARE
Willard Saulsbury

FLORIDA
Duncan U. Fletcher

ILLINOIS
James Hamilton Lewis
Lawrence Y. Sherman

INDIANA
Harry Stewart New
James E. Watson

IOWA
Albert B. Cummins
William S. Kenyon

KANSAS
Charles Curtis

LOUISIANA
Walter Guion
Joseph E. Ransdell

MAINE
Bert M. Fernald
Frederick Hale

MARYLAND
Joseph Irwin France

MASSACHUSETTS
Henry Cabot Lodge
John W. Weeks

MICHIGAN
Charles E. Townsend

MINNESOTA
Frank B. Kellogg
Knute Nelson

MISSISSIPPI
James K. Vardaman
John Sharp Williams

MISSOURI
James A. Reed
Xenophon P. Wifley

MONTANA
Henry L. Myers

NEBRASKA
Gilbert M. Hitchcock

NEVADA
Key Pittman

14

NEW HAMPSHIRE
  Irving W. Drew

NEW JERSEY
  Joseph S. Frelinghuysen

NEW MEXICO
  Albert B. Fall

NEW YORK
  William M. Calder
  James W. Wadsworth, Jr.

NORTH CAROLINA
  Lee Slater Overman
  F. M. Simmons

NORTH DAKOTA
  Porter J. McCumber

OKLAHOMA
  Thomas P. Gore
  Robert L. Owen

OREGON
  George E. Chamberlain
  Charles L. McNary

PENNSYLVANIA
  Boies Penrose

RHODE ISLAND
  Le Baron B. Colt

SOUTH CAROLINA
  Christie Benet

SOUTH DAKOTA
  Thomas Sterling

TENNESSEE
  Kenneth D. McKellar

TEXAS
  Charles A. Culberson
  Morris Sheppard

UTAH
  William H. King
  Reed Smoot

VERMONT
  W. P. Dillingham

WASHINGTON
  Miles Poindexter
  Wesley L. Jones

WEST VIRGINIA
  Howard Sutherland

WISCONSIN
  Irvine L. Lenroot

WYOMING
  John B. Kendrick
  Francis E. Warren

REPRESENTATIVES*

ALABAMA
William B. Bankhead
John L. Burnett
Oscar L. Gray
Fred L. Blackmon
S. Hubert Dent
J. Thomas Heflin
William B. Oliver

ARKANSAS
Thaddeus H. Caraway
Henderson M. Jacoway
William A. Oldfield
John N. Tillman

CALIFORNIA
Denver S. Church
Charles F. Curry
Eneris A. Hayes
William Kettner
Clarence F. Lea
Henry Z. Osborne
John E. Raker

CONNECTICUT
Richard P. Freeman
James P. Glynn
Augustine Lonergan
Schuyler Merritt
John Q. Tilson

COLORADO
Benjamin C. Hilliard
Edward Keating
Edward T. Taylor
Charles B. Timberlake

DELAWARE
Albert F. Polk

FLORIDA
Frank Clark
Walter Kehoe

GEORGIA
Charles R. Crisp
William W. Larsen
Frank Park

HAWAII
J. Kunio Kalanianaole

IDAHO
Burton L. French
Addison T. Smith

ILLINOIS
Edward E. Denison
Charles E. Fuller
Thomas Gallagher
William J. Graham
Clifford Ireland
Niels Juul
Medill McCormick
William B. McKinley
Martin B. Madden
William E. Mason
Henry T. Rainey
John W. Rainey
William A. Rodenberg
Adolph J. Sabath
John A. Sterling
Loren E. Wheeler

*Includes Delegates from Hawaii, the Philippine Islands and Porto Rico.

16

INDIANA
William E. Cox
Henry A. Barnhart
George K. Denton
Louis W. Fairfield
Merrill Moores
Fred S. Purnell
Everett Sanders
Albert H. Vestal
William R. Wood

IOWA
William R. Green
Harry E. Hull
Horace M. Towner
Frank P. Woods

KANSAS
Daniel R. Anthony, Jr.
W. A. Ayres
Philip P. Campbell
Guy T. Helvering
Edward C. Little

KENTUCKY
James C. Cantrill
Swagar Sherley

LOUISIANA
H. Garland Dupré
Albert Estopinal
Whitmell P. Martin
John T. Watkins

MAINE
Louis B. Goodall
Wallace H. White, Jr.

MARYLAND
Charles P. Coady
Jesse D. Price
Frederick N. Zihlman

MASSACHUSETTS
Frederick W. Dallinger
Alvan T. Fuller
James A. Gallivan
Frederick H. Gillett
William S. Greene
Wilfred W. Lufkin
Richard Olney
Calvin D. Paige
John J. Rogers
George Holden Tinkham
Allen T. Treadway
William W. Venable
Joseph Walsh

MICHIGAN
Samuel W. Beakes
Gilbert A. Currie
Frank E. Doremus
Joseph W. Fordney
Edward L. Hamilton
Patrick H. Kelley
Carl E. Mapes

MINNESOTA
Harold Knutson
Clarence B. Miller
Thomas D. Schall
Halvor Steenerson

MISSISSIPPI
Thomas Upton Sisson

MISSOURI
Charles F. Booher
William P. Borland
Champ Clark
Leonidas C. Dyer
Walter L. Hensley
Milton A. Romjue

17

MONTANA
Jeanette Rankin

NEBRASKA
Moses J. Kinkaid
Charles C. Lobeck
Charles H. Sloan
Dan V. Stephens

NEW HAMPSHIRE
Sherman E. Burroughs

NEW JERSEY
Isaac Bachrach
William J. Browning
Edward W. Gray
Elijah C. Hutchinson
Frederick R. Lehlbach
John R. Ramsey

NEW YORK
John F. Carew
Walter M. Chandler
W. E. Cleary
S. Wallace Dempsey
Jerome F. Donovan
Benjamin L. Fairchild
Joseph U. Flynn
George B. Francis
Anthony J. Griffin
Reuben L. Haskell
Florello H. La Guardia
George R. Lunn
James P. Maher
Luther W. Mott
Edmund Platt
Daniel J. Riordan
Frederick W. Rowe
Isaac Siegel
Charles Bennett Smith
Thomas F. Smith
Homer P. Snyder

NEW YORK—*Continued*
Christopher D. Sullivan
Oscar William Swift
William F. Waldon
Charles E. Ward

NORTH CAROLINA
Hannibal L. Godwin
John H. Small
Charles W. Stedman
Zebulon Weaver

NORTH DAKOTA
J. M. Baer
George M. Young

OHIO
Clement Brumbaugh
Horatio C. Claypool
Robert Crosser
Henry I. Emerson
Simeon D. Fess
Warren Gard
William Gordon
David A. Hollingsworth
Roscoe C. McCulloch
Isaac R. Sherwood
John S. Snook
Benjamin F. Welty

OKLAHOMA
Charles D. Carter
Tom D. McKeown
Dick T. Morgan

OREGON
Willis C. Hawley

PENNSYLVANIA
Earl H. Beshlin
Guy E. Campbell
Henry A. Clark
Peter E. Costello

PENNSYLVANIA—*Continued*
Thomas S. Crago
George P. Darrow
George W. Edmonds
John R. Farr
B. K. Focht
Manlon M. Garland
George Scott Graham
M. Clyde Kelly
Edgar R. Kriess
Aaron S. Kreider
J. Hampton Moore
John M. Morin
Edward E. Robbins
John M. Rose
Bruce F. Sterling
Nathan N. Strong
Henry W. Temple
Thomas W. Templeton
William S. Vare
Henry W. Watson

PHILIPPINE ISLANDS
Jaime C. De Veyra
Teodoro R. Yangco

PORTO RICO
Felix Cordova Davila

RHODE ISLAND
George F. O'Shaunessy
Walter R. Stiness

SOUTH CAROLINA
Samuel J. Nicholls
William F. Stevenson

SOUTH DAKOTA
Charles H. Dillon
Harry L. Gandy

TENNESSEE
Richard W. Austin
Joseph W. Byrnes
Finis J. Garrett
William C. Houston
Cordell Hull
Lemuel P. Padgett

TEXAS
Eugene Black
Thomas L. Blanton
James P. Buchanon
Joe H. Eagle
Rufus Hardy
Jeff. McLemore
Joseph J. Mansfield
James L. Slayden
James C. Wilson

VERMONT
Frank L. Greene

VIRGINIA
Edward W. Saunders
Walter A. Watson

WASHINGTON
C. C. Dill
Lindley H. Hadley
Albert Johnson
John F. Miller
John A. Moon

WEST VIRGINIA
Edward Cooper
Adam B. Littlepage
Stuart F. Reed

WISCONSIN
Edward E. Browne
William J. Cary
David G. Classon
Henry A. Cooper
John J. Esch

WISCONSIN—*Continued*
James A. Frear
John M. Nelson
Edward Voight

WYOMING
Frank W. Mondell

SUMMARY

Members of Congress from whom statements have been received:

Senators	61	From 43 states.
Representatives	239	From 44 states and three territories.
Total	300	

Statements of
United States Senators

By Senator John H. Bankhead,
Of Alabama.

"I am in hearty accord with the suggestion to re-establish in Palestine a Jewish National Center. The movement has assumed such proportions, the time apparently has appeared to put into execution the request desired of the leaders of the Jewish people for a number of years to re-establish themselves with national headquarters in Palestine.

"I am ready to co-operate in every way I can to that end." **In Hearty Accord**

(Signed) "J. H. BANKHEAD."

By Senator Marcus A. Smith,
Of Arizona.

"If it will be of help to the Jewish race, I am for Zionism, and stand ready and willing at all times to help the oppressed Jews or any other oppressed people, whenever opportunity presents itself." **Ready to Aid.**

(Signed) "M. A. SMITH."

By Senator William F. Kirby,
Of Arkansas.

"If it is the purpose to re-establish a nation by bringing together the oppressed peoples of this race from other lands, its achievement would be a great blessing, but unless from sentimental and religious motives, I discover no especial reason for the location chosen. There are better lands and conditions for the development of a prosperous and happy people in other governments long passed the experimentation stage. The people of this race are desirable citizens in our own country, and why waste time and effort in an attempt to re-establish them in a country in which we have no material interest and where their environment would not be comparable even for generations with the conditions they now enjoy?" **Blessing for Oppressed— Other Lands Better.**

(Signed) "WM. F. KIRBY."

23

By Senator Joseph T. Robinson,
Of Arkansas.

Zionism Romantic but Practical.

"The proposed establishment of a Homeland in Palestine for persecuted Jews is both romantic and practicable. Throughout many centuries the Jewish race has experienced envy and suffered persecution in almost every land. Now that a better day for humanity is dawning, it seems appropriate that this great people should provide themselves with a home, should assemble in a country where their peculiar institutions may become dominant and where they may enjoy liberty unrestricted.

Liberal Gentiles Co-operate.

"Many liberal Gentiles heartily co-operate in this great movement and express the hope that it may succeed."

(Signed)   "Jos. T. Robinson."

By Senator James D. Phelan,
Of California.

"From the character of the men supporting the Advantages of Restoration. Zionist movement, I believe that it is entitled to the most careful consideration. These men, several of my personal acquaintance, like Justice Brandeis, and David Lubin, are men of vision and imagination. They would restore the Jewish nation with its glorious traditions, literary, heroic and religious, and bring the Hebrew race to a full realization of its power and possibilities. It would primarily be for the benefit of the Jews, less fortunate than those who have now the opportunity to develop themselves under American institutions.

"All over the world the Jews are scattered, and are Sympathetic Environment for Jews. unwelcome guests in many lands. Why should not these people be brought under the sympathetic influence of a restored and constructive Judaism?

"Men who are purely commercial in their senti- Not Utopian. ment, might regard such a plan as Utopian, but viewing this question historically and seeing the possibilities of a nation re-established in Palestine, which is naturally the most fitting and inspiring spot, consecrated in the Jewish mind by the triumphs and tribulations of a proud people. Now, as a race, without a country, I would give them this word of encouragement from the poet: 'Dream bravely and well, and your dreams shall be prophets.'

"I do not know in what manner the United States, Will Urge Government Support. through the action of Congress, might best advance this great idea and give it actuality, but I shall be pleased when the matter comes up for discussion, to urge in a broad and general way, co-operation with other nations. Yet I feel that our American institutions are so favorable to men of every race and religion that we should be careful not to disturb our own Jewish citizens, but regard the movement as a humanitarian one to bring equal opportunity to all those whom the United States can not shelter, and, at the same time, create a home for a nationality that has proven itself indestructible and worthy of a local habitation and a name."

(Signed) "James D. Phelan."

The American War Congress and Zionism

By Senator Charles S. Thomas,
Of Colorado.

Acquisition of Homeland Dignifies Position.
"Having given the subject some consideration since the capture of Jerusalem by the British forces, I do not hesitate to give it my unqualified endorsement. I believe, that the status of the Jewish people the world over would be improved and their rights more fully recognized, if, like people of other races, they enjoyed a fixed national territory, possessing the attributes of a modern government, and recognized as a member of the family of nations. The representation which this condition would give through the interchange of envoys and ministers to other countries, and the consciousness of the collective citizenship of the race, endowed with the attributes of a nation could not be otherwise than beneficial and elevating to the humblest member of the race. Such a movement would do for the Jews what the rehabilitation of Greece has accomplished for the Greeks within the short space of a century.

Independence of Palestine Indispensable to Peace.
"Politically, the conversion of Palestine into an independent nation, in view of the boundless and unscrupulous ambitions of Germany, would seem to be an indispensable element in assuring future peace to the world. This obvious situation doubtless inspired the announcement of the British Government, November 2nd, last, albeit, the sentimental side of the proposal may have been quite as persuasive. A compact, powerful and self-governing people in Asia Minor, thrust between the German-controlled Turkish dominions to the North and the Suez Canal, with Arabia to the South would do much to check the tide of aggression from that quarter and safeguard the great sea route through the Suez Canal to India.

Among War's Crowning Benefits.
"Aside from these considerations is the one which presumably appeals to the Jews more powerfully than all of them. I refer to that national longing which the race has entertained ever since its dispersion by the Romans, which has survived persecution, adversity, and all of the misery of centuries. The re-establishment of a Jewish Nation upon the site of its former home will

satisfy that aspiration and constitute a monument of justice—albeit a tardy one—to the heroic and indomitable persistence of Judaism throughout the centuries. This, of itself, will, I think, guarantee the success of the enterprise, to which posterity will point as one of the crowning benefits of the world's greatest war.

"Although the foregoing statement would seem to constitute a collective reply to your several queries, I will nevertheless also make these categorical answers: *Zionism Should be Encouraged.*

"I approve the Declaration of our Allies upon the Zionist question, for the reasons above outlined.

"I think that our own Government should officially express its accord with these declarations through an appropriate joint resolution by Congress to that effect.

"I think the effort of the Jewish people to establish a national home in Palestine should be encouraged at all times."

(Signed)   "C. S. Thomas."

By Senator George P. McLean,
Of Connecticut.

"I have read with interest, the views of Senators Lodge* and Cummins** and heartily approve everything they say, and while I should be glad to see Congress act in the matter, it seems to me that the subject is one upon which the Executive should take the initiative." *Approves— Initiative for Executive.*

(Signed)   "Geo. P. McLean."

---

* See statement by Senator Lodge, page 43.
** See statement by Senator Cummins, page 33.

By Senator Willard Saulsbury,
Of Delaware.

President Pro Tempore of the Senate of the United States.

World's Payment of Debt.

"The Declarations of Great Britain, France, Italy, and our other Allies favoring the establishment in Palestine of a National Jewish Centre is a happy fulfillment of the prophesies of the Bible. These Pronouncements also mark, in a most fitting manner and at the opportune moment, the debt that the world is paying to the Jews for their age-long persecutions. The free peoples of the earth are now causing to bring about the freedom of the Jewish nation.

Revival of Hebrew Culture.

"With this re-establishment in Palestine, the language of the old Testament will again be revived and the great Hebrew culture and civilization will again find its natural channels for expression and development.

Deserve War's Democratic Fruits.

"The Jews have contributed in treasures and in blood to every belligerent in this contest. They have suffered in this struggle equally with any other participant. They thus justly deserve the democratic fruits of this war. Nothing would be as fitting and proper, and no other means would solve their problem more thoroughly, than their re-establishment as a nation on their ancient land. This national rebirth of the Jew strikes at the core of the entire question.

Action by United States.

"With the true spirit of rights of nations for self-assertion and self-determination, the United States, through the proper Government agency, may declare itself in favor of Zionism. I feel certain that this time is not far distant."

(Signed)   "WILLARD SAULSBURY."

By Senator Duncan U. Fletcher,
Of Florida.

Sympathizes with Jewish Homeland.

"I cordially sympathize with your efforts to establish a Jewish Homeland in Palestine in accordance with the official declarations of England, France and Italy.

"I wish the friends of the undertaking every success."

(Signed)   "DUNCAN U. FLETCHER."

28

By Senator James Hamilton Lewis,
Of Illinois.

"My reason for approving the establishment of Zion as a national habitation of the Jewish people, is not to encourage them to leave the country of their residence, nor to insinuate to them that such is desirable from any point. It is, that as every people and every nationality has some place which they call the original home of their fathers, to deny to the Jewish people a similar privilege would make a discrimination that could not be justified. *Anti-Zionism Would Be Discrimination.*

"The establishment of Zion gives the Jewish people their ancient home and is no more in its inception than of a family purchasing the old house where their parents were born or where they themselves were born. I wholly approve of those Jews who wish to make this establishment at Zion, and I am gratified that my government and the government of other parts of the world will recognize this movement as not a race movement nor a religious movement, but a national movement of a people who along with other peoples of the world have a right to a motherland and a mother home. *A Homeland an Inherent Right.*

"And about Palestine, more appropriate than in any part of the world, is the natural and just location of the Jewish people when they come to establish their home of sentiment and their place of history." *Palestine Most Appropriate.*

(Signed)   "Jas. Hamilton Lewis."

**By Senator Lawrence Y. Sherman,
Of Illinois.**

Jewish
Homeland
Practical.

"The Zionist undertaking for a national home for the Jewish people in Palestine is a laudable one. The declarations of the governments of Great Britain, France and Italy officially stated, favoring the rights of smaller nationalities, give fairly the substance of the movement. The Jewish State founded upon the principles of toleration and civil justice would enable those of the Hebrew race who have been the victims of oppression in the Old World to form a country where the future peace league of nations could recognize and extend its protection. My hope would be that it would eventually become a place of refuge of the countries that persecute or discriminate against this race. I believe a dawning of a better day with more universal toleration and a keener sense of justice is at hand. A Jewish homeland would be a practical step in relief."

(Signed) "LAWRENCE Y. SHERMAN."

By Senator Harry Stewart New,
Of Indiana.

"Of course, I am heartily in favor of the Balfour Declaration for a Jewish homeland in the Holy Land. I certainly do think that the Jews ought to have a National Government of their own; which appears to be the ambitions of so many of your people. I am confident that if the Jews, as events appear to indicate, will form such a Government in the land of their forefathers, that it will, indeed, be a well conducted State. I think that it would be an inspiration to them, and would also aid the Jewish people the world over both physically and spiritually. The formation of a Jewish State would arouse and bring out in your people many dormant qualities; it would prove an inspiration to your race along lines which, among others, were denied to them partly through prejudice. They would certainly be quick to use altered conditions advantageously. *Should Inspire All Jews.*

"Furthermore, I sincerely believe that the British Declaration has put forward documentarily the fact that the problem of the Jewish State is to be included as one of the aims of the War. Let me emphasize that I *do* think that the Jews ought to be among the small nations, the assurance of whose safety is one of the main purposes of the War. I am convinced in my belief that all peoples should be given an opportunity to govern themselves, provided they are capable of self-government, and no one would question the ability of the Jewish people to govern themselves. History has shown this quality in the Jews, and all of us know it well, directly and indirectly. *War Fought for Small Nations.*

"I do not believe it at all improbable that, should conditions warrant, America may be induced to become the protectorate and be the guarantor for the Jewish State, at least during the first period. This may come about through international agreement, for the benefit and protection of every one concerned. Some such scheme would insure absolute justice to all." *American Protectorate of Jewish State.*

(Signed)   "HARRY S. NEW."

3   31

**By Senator James E. Watson,
Of Indiana.**

In Accord
with Dec-
larations.

"As far as I am concerned, I find myself in entire accord with the declarations of England, France and Italy on the Zionist proposition. I am most decidedly of the opinion that Palestine, and in fact all the places made holy by the presence of Jesus of Nazareth and, therefore, sacred to the world, should be forever removed from Turkish control.

Place Land
under
Jewish Rule.

"In my judgment, the best way to accomplish this desired result, is to place the entire country under the rule of the Jews. The sacred traditions that cluster around Jerusalem are of supreme interest to civilization, but naturally they are of paramount importance to the Jews of the world, because Jerusalem is the city of the Jews, and they naturally feel as if they should be its guardians and likewise the keepers and rulers of all the holy places of ancient Palestine.

Equal
Rights
to All.

"I take it for granted, of course, that such a rule by such a people would not in anywise prejudice either the civil or religious rights of non-Jewish people, for the Jews are lovers of liberty and, having been so mercilessly persecuted by many of the nations of the world, would naturally shrink from pursuing any such course toward any other people.

Favors
Action by
Congress.

"I take it for granted that the Jewish people of the country are in favor of this movement and personally, I know of no reason why a resolution should not be passed in Congress in favor of the movement you have in contemplation."

(Signed)   "James E. Watson."

By Senator Albert B. Cummins,
Of Iowa.

"With the spirit of the British statement I am in entire sympathy. My reason for looking upon the subject from a different angle is based partially upon the vagueness of the British Declaration. I have been unable to understand fully the meaning of the words 'a National Home,' as used in the British expression. If the purpose is simply to promote a settlement in Palestine of men and women of the Jewish race, without regard to the government under which they shall live, the proposal, while it may be a very worthy one, falls far short of my conception of the world-wide movement. *In Sympathy with Declaration.*

"If it be the desire of the Jewish people themselves, I am in favor of lending our national influence toward the establishment in Palestine of a government; that is to say, an independent state, sustained and controlled by men and women of that blood. It was with this thought in my mind that I asked you for information respecting the capacity of the territory called Palestine to support a population large enough to give dignity and permanence to a sovereignty of that character. *For Independent Jewish State.*

"The Jewish people have had a career so unique and wonderful in every way that they richly deserve the assistance of the civilized world in carrying forward such an experiment. Through the chaos of the earlier ages, and through all the injustice of modern times, they have persisted, and demonstrated in the most striking manner the virility of the race. They ought to have all the opportunity which the great powers of the earth can extend to them, to show their fitness for self-government. *Jews Fully Deserve It.*

"You will observe that my view is more comprehensive than a mere 'National Home' although it may well be that Mr. Balfour, the British Secretary of State for Foreign Affairs, employed these words in the broader sense. If he did, I wholly approve of his Declaration, and am earnestly in favor of a like statement on the part of the Government of the United States. If he did not, I am in favor of action by our *Action by Our Government.*

33

Government that will express in proper form the sentiments I have so briefly outlined.

Same Right As Other Races.

"I want to see in the world, as the outcome of the war in which we are engaged, a Jewish State with the same right of existence and development as it is hoped will be given to other races which desire to hold together and live together for their mutual happiness, safety and growth."

(Signed)   "ALBERT B. CUMMINS."

By Senator William S. Kenyon,
Of Iowa.

Favors Jewish Homeland.

"I am earnestly in favor of this plan for a Jewish homeland in Palestine, and certainly trust that this desired consummation may come out of this war."

(Signed)   "W. S. KENYON."

By Senator Charles Curtis,
Of Kansas.

Entitled to Self-Governing State.

"I heartily agree to and approve of the Declarations of England, France and Italy in regard to a Jewish homeland in Palestine. I hope in due time the United States will take a similar stand on this question. These long oppressed people should be given an opportunity of working out and determining their own future in a homeland of their own."

(Signed)   "CHARLES CURTIS."

The American War Congress and Zionism

By Senator Walter Guion,
Of Louisiana.

"Many centuries ago Cyrus, King of Persia, issued a proclamation permitting the return of the Jews to Palestine, there to re-establish their old National Home. Last year the Government of Great Britain and all of those associated as allies, with her, issued similar proclamations which were well received throughout the universe. Historically, therefore, these Zionist Declarations may well be regarded as among the positive acts of the War and, doubtless, will be so pronounced by future generations. *(Cyrus Proclamation and British Declaration.)*

"I do not hesitate to declare that I am heartily in accord with these Declarations of our Allies for a Jewish State in Palestine, for it may well be said of the Jews that one of their strongest traits is this great National ambition. *(National Ambition Admirable.)*

"This worthy movement includes among its supporters, so many of our best citizens that it speaks in strong and unequivocal terms for its thorough Americanism. *(Thorough Americanism of Movement.)*

"We have before us, in our everyday life, constant evidence of the many achievements of the Jewish race in every line of human endeavor, and it is not too much to expect, that with all of their forceful characteristics brought into play, re-established Israel will become a model Nation." *(To Become Model Nation.)*

(Signed) "WALTER GUION."

By Senator Joseph E. Ransdell,
Of Louisiana.

Will Vote for Resolution.
"I am heartily in favor of the official declarations of England, France and Italy on the Zionist question, and shall gladly vote for an appropriate resolution by Congress favoring the establishment of a Jewish National Centre in Palestine, provided ample guarantees are furnished for protecting in all civil and religious rights the Fellahin who have been its peasant farmers for centuries, and the many Christians who have lived there for generations.

Jewish Republic under Protectorate.
"In this period of new nations when the world is being thrilled by the death agonies of old Empires and the birth of strong young democracies, it seems peculiarly appropriate that a Jewish Republic should be founded in Palestine under the aegis of some powerful country which will do for it what the United States is doing so nobly for Cuba.

Loyal Citizens— Proud of Heritage.
"No race on earth except the Jews has maintained for two thousand years, while scattered over the face of the globe, its separate and distinct language, nationality and religion. All others have blended so thoroughly with the people among whom they lived that in three or four generations their racial characteristics and national traits were lost. The Jew of today, though for the past two hundred years a citizen of Italy, France, Great Britain, or the United States, and loyal in every fibre of his being to the land of his birth, is nevertheless proud to be known and recognized as a Jew. He traces his ancestry in direct line for five thousand years, and numbers among his forbears kings, warriors, lawmakers, historians, orators, poets and leaders in everything great and noble who lived when the founders of races who now rule the world were untaught savages.

Jewish Contribution to World.
"Palestine was the home of the Jews—indeed their birthplace, and only real home—for three thousand years before the Christian Era, and from that centre emanated laws, philosophies, and moral teachings that greatly benefitted mankind. Then came a long period of trial, suffering and wandering in many lands, so much so, that

36

Jewish names appear in the annals of all countries, and
often receive the most honorable mention. Palestine was
no longer occupied and ruled by Jews; strangers trod
the scenes and tilled the soil so long and honorably held
by them; and at this moment there are doubtless more
Christians and Moslems in the Holy Land than Jews,
while in several other countries there are many more
Jews than in Palestine.

"Throughout all these ages and vicissitudes, Jews
have hoped and dreamed of returning to the Promised
Land, making it flow as of old with milk and honey,
setting up a government of, by and for Jews, restoring the
Hebrew language, and again taking the place among Nations so long held by them. It is a laudable, proper ambition which should be assisted by the freedom loving
people of our Republic in every way.

Zionism Laudable Ambition— Deserves Assistance.

"The establishment of such a Jewish state in Palestine
as we would have every reason to expect from a people
so frugal, persistent, energetic, wise, and forceful as the
Jews, would be a great boon to that part of the world.
It would aid materially in restoring Syria and Mesopotamia to their former commanding positions as populous,
wealthy, progressive countries, and be a strong bulwark
against the insidious depredations of the Turk. I am
firmly convinced that, entirely aside from sentiments
of justice and sympathy for Jews, it would be extremely
wise and statesmanlike to establish and support, until it
could stand alone, a Jewish Republic in Palestine."

Statesman-like Disposi-tion of Palestine.

(Signed)   "Jos. E. Ransdell."

By Senator Bert M. Fernald,
Of Maine.

Approves
Declaration.

"I heartily approve the recent Declarations made by England, France and Italy relative to the Zionist question.

Recognizes
Jewish
Claim.

"At this time, when our great Nation and its Allies are prosecuting a war professedly for the freedom of oppressed nationalities, it seems to me peculiarly fitting and proper to recognize the claim of the Jewish peoples to be permitted to establish a permanent home in Palestine, where in the future they may maintain their racial integrity.

"Jerusalem is the logical city for the Jews; and I should be glad to see the United States take action in line with the British Declaration."

(Signed)   "BERT W. FERNALD."

By Senator Frederick Hale,
Of Maine.

Justice and
World's
Sacred
Duty.

"I thoroughly approve of the action of our Allies on the Zionist question. The restoration to the Jews of their old home land is an act of justice that the world owes to them. It is very unfortunate that this act has been delayed for so many centuries, in which the Jewish people have endured untold suffering. By returning Palestine to the Jews, the Allied Powers are carrying out a sacred duty. This war is bound to cause many changes, and pre-eminent among these changes will be the one in the status of the Jewish people. I shall be glad to be of any service in helping this just cause."

(Signed)   "FREDERICK HALE."

38

By Senator Joseph Irwin France,
Of Maryland.

"I am very much interested in the Zionist movement and I will look forward with hope and confidence to its success. The re-establishment of a Jewish Homeland in Palestine would be hailed by men of progressive thought as a great event in the history of Civilization. It is a cause for which the Jewish peoples in every land may work with enthusiastic devotion without any sacrifice of their love and loyalty for the country of which they have become citizens.

"My views upon this subject are more fully expressed in a brief address which I made at a Zionist meeting in Baltimore sometime since, from which you may prefer to take extracts and a copy of which is enclosed.

"I wish you every success as you continue your work for the realization of your great ideal."

(Signed)   "JOSEPH I. FRANCE."

Zionists Loyal Citizens.

The speech of Senator France, delivered on February 18, 1917, follows:

"A JEWISH RE-DEDICATION.

Preservation
of Jewish
Ideals.

"Through all the centuries from the dawn of civilization the Hebrew people have lived on; they have witnessed the birth, the rise and the fall of many empires, and the extinction of many races of men; they have lived on, preserved by a special providence and through all the years of their remarkable history, priceless gifts, matchless contributions and new spiritual revelations have been made, by them, and through them, to humanity; and to the civilization of the world its indispensable gifts.

"It is possible to imagine this world without the contributions which some nations have made to history, but I cannot conceive of this world as it would have been without Palestine, and without that great spiritual light with which the whole world has been illumined; a light which has come through the genius and mission of the Hebrew people.

World's
Heritage
from
Ancient
State.

"I cannot conceive of a world without the sacred books with their inspiring national and spiritual history. I cannot imagine a world without the law and the great words of the Hebrew prophets, which have come ringing with authority down through all the centuries as true and as potent today as they were when spoken. What would the world be without the Psalms, sung first in Palestine and then in ever-widening circles with the passage of the centuries, by an ever-swelling chorus joined now by men of every land and tribe, a chorus which shall yet rise higher, ascending as a mighty paean of praise when all the peoples of the earth shall unite to sing the infinite Fatherhood of God and the unlimited brotherhood of man.

Cultural
Revival.

"I do not feel that I am competent to discuss all of the phases of the Zionist question. Some hold, I know, that this great Zionist movement must lose some of its significance with the inevitable decline of the anti-Semitic sentiments and feelings; other contend that the

40

great works of the Jews for the world must be done
within the countries of which they are now such an
important and integral part. I have no doubt myself
that anti-Semitic feelings and sentiments must decline
and ultimately disappear completely with the progress
of civilization. I am convinced also that it would be an
irreparable loss to the world to have any large proportion of your people leave their present homes, in the
enlightened countries, to take up residences in Palestine,
and yet I do believe the Zionist movement to be something far more significant than a mere effort to establish
a refuge in Palestine for the oppressed Jews of Russia
and of Southern Europe, desirable and important as such
a movement as that, in itself, would be. I believe that
its most thoughtful advocates see in this movement not
only the securing of a national home, the reclamation of
Palestine, the awakening of an interest in the revival of
Jewish agriculture, language, literature and art, but,
more than all, the rededication of the Jewish people
themselves to the great spiritual conceptions and ideals of
the past, to that lofty spiritual altruism which is the very
essence of their religion.

"We all stand in danger, particularly in this country, **Spiritual Rededication.**
with our great prosperity, of sinking into materialism.
Every man wants to play a man's part, to heroically
meet and overcome the problems and difficulties of daily
life, and he naturally desires those material things which
are not only enjoyable in themselves, but which are also
the outward symbols of success and victory. Our greatest menace today is that materialism and paganism,
which have ever been in the past so destructive to national life. We must keep our spiritual eyes open,
remembering ever that 'where there is no vision the
people perish.' Spiritual vision is more important than
material possession.

"Our great Republic needs the very best that is in **Quickening of Spirit Will Benefit America.**
every Jewish citizen; his patriotism, his great practical
ability, his spiritual insight and this most significant
Zionist movement, which cannot succeed without a re-
newed devotion on your part to your best traditions and

41

ideals, should be a means toward that re-awakened and quickened spirituality of which all of us in America stand in such great need.

Palestine Spiritual Reservoir.

"Palestine was a great spiritual reservoir from which pure, sweet, healing, cooling streams were poured out over the barren, fevered lands desolate under the blighting touch of polytheism, paganism, and materialism; and those lands purified and fructified by the life-giving streams brought forth justice, liberty, civilization and all the blessed fruits of the spirit. May that great spiritual reservoir be rebuilded not only upon the beautiful hills and in the pleasant valleys of Palestine, but in every land where the children of Israel are gathered together.

From Jehuda Halevi.

"I admire that magnificent and immortal ode in which your great physician, poet and modern Psalmist, Jehuda Halevi, sang of Zion:

" 'Oh, who will lead me on
 To seek the posts where, in far distant years,
The angels in their glory dawned upon
 Thy messengers and seers?'

"But the longing of his heart for the physical and temporal restoration of Zion did not prevent his realization that in a great true sense Zion is not a place but a spirit, and he wrote that beautiful poem-prayer which we all would do well to make our own.

" 'Oh! would that I might be
A servant unto Thee,
Thou God, by all adored.
Then, though by friends outcast,
Thy hand would hold me fast,
And draw me near to Thee, my King and Lord.' "

The American War Congress and Zionism

By Senator Henry Cabot Lodge,
Of Massachusetts.

"I entirely approve the declarations of England, France and Italy on the Zionist question. I favor the declarations because it seems to me that Palestine and the Holy Places of both the Christian and Jewish religions should be forever removed from Turkish control. Jerusalem is the city of the Jews and they would be the natural guardians of the city and of the Holy Places,—it being of course understood, as Mr. Balfour says, that nothing would be done which would prejudice the civil and religious rights of non-Jewish people in Palestine, which I am sure would be protected and conserved in every way by the Zionists. *(Jews Natural Palestine Guardians.)*

"I should be glad to see action by the United States Government in line with the British Declaration. The question is one upon which action must be looked for first from the Executive, under our system of Government; but personally I should favor the adoption of an appropriate resolution by Congress in favor of the establishment in Palestine of a Jewish National Centre. *(Favors Action by United States.)*

"I feel that the effort of the Jewish people to establish a National Home in Palestine is not only natural but in all ways to be desired." *(Zionism Natural and Desirable.)*

(Signed) "HENRY C. LODGE."

43

By Senator John W. Weeks,
Of Massachusetts.

Place
Palestine
under
Zionist
Protection.

"If I understand correctly the declaration of England, France, and Italy, it has my entire approval. It seems to me that the holy places of the Jewish religion should be removed from Turkish control. That is an anomalous condition which should not be allowed to continue, and I should be glad to see action taken by our Government in approval of the policy of placing Palestine under the protection of the Zionists. Of course, you understand that the initiative in such matters must come from the Executive branch of our Government, but in case any legislative action is required it will have my hearty support."   (Signed)   "JOHN W. WEEKS."

By Senator Charles E. Townsend,
Of Michigan.

Restore
Palestine to
Jews.

"From the newspaper reports of the Zionist movement having for its object the establishment in Palestine of a national home for the Jewish people, I find myself in hearty sympathy with the proposition. I am not prepared to state what action, if any, the American Congress should take in reference to the matter. I have felt that it was unwise for the United States to take any official action during the pendency of the war on the question of disposition of foreign countries or peoples. It probably will be necessary to consider this question at the international peace table. I venture the hope, however, that it will be found advisable and wise to divest the Turk from all control over the historic and revered Judea including Constantinople and I can think of nothing more appropriate than the restoration of this country to its ancient inhabitants—the Jews. I hope the movement will succeed."   (Signed)   "CHAS. E. TOWNSEND."

By Senator Frank B. Kellogg,
Of Minnesota.

"I am in entire sympathy with the purposes of the **Autonomous Government in Palestine.** Zionist movement and with the view of the British Government, as expressed by Mr. Balfour and, as I understand, endorsed by the French and Italian Governments, and by President Wilson. I approve it, not only as a movement looking to the settlement of Palestine by the Jews, but in the end when such settlement shall have reached a point to justify it, the establishment of an autonomous government. This government, of course, should protect the civil and religious rights of all non-Jewish inhabitants.

"I understand that Jewish colonization has already **National and Cultural Revival Creditable.** progressed to a point where its success is demonstrated. That for the first time in centuries the Hebrew language is being taught and is the medium of intercourse by these people. It is a remarkable tribute to this ancient race, whose civilization was old before Rome dominated the Western world, that through more than twenty centuries they have been able to preserve their virility, their culture and their religious and racial characteristics.

"We all know in the struggle for position amid con- **Advantage of Possessing Homeland.** tending races of the world, the advantage of having a country one can call his own, and this advantage is immeasurably heightened by the fact that this country is being established in the ancient seat of the race.

"I do not, of course, expect that large numbers of **A Longing of Centuries.** Jews will leave this country, where they have all the advantages of our enlightened institutions, to live in Palestine, but I believe that it will satisfy a longing that has never ceased to exist through their struggle during all these centuries." (Signed) "FRANK B. KELLOGG."

**By Senator Knute Nelson,
Of Minnesota.**

Sentiment
Commend-
able—Land
Unfertile.

"I can very well understand why, as a matter of sentiment, the Jews would like to settle, reclaim, and reorganize Palestine. This sentiment is highly to be commended, but my understanding is that Palestine is, to some extent, a semi-arid country, hilly and somewhat barren, and not what we would call here in America a good agricultural country. For that reason, it seems to me that it is not a good plan to get the poor people of Jewish descent, who are anxious to make their living by farming, to go to that country.

Favors
Jewish
Realization

"There are many places here in America that would be better for farms and homes. But, however this may be, I shall certainly be glad to see the Jewish people occupy and control Palestine.

"Yours very truly,

(Signed)   "KNUTE NELSON."

46

By Senator James K. Vardaman,
Of Mississippi.

"I can scarcely conceive of an American imbued **All Americans Should Approve.** with the spirit of freedom and informed of the history of the Jewish people, who could fail to approve most heartily the sentiment expressed by the Honorable Arthur J. Balfour, Secretary of State for Foreign Affairs of the British Government, with reference to the establishment in Palestine of a National Home for the Jewish people.

"That the Government of the United States will use **Jews Entitled to Homeland.** its best endeavors to facilitate and encourage that achievement, I have not the least doubt. That the race that gave the world The Great Exemplar of the civilized nations and which has contributed so much in other ways to the moral and material upbuilding of mankind is entitled to this National Home, protected in the enjoyment of absolute autonomy, unproscribed and uninterfered with, is a matter of common justice.

"I can imagine the Republic of Palestine as being a **Would Encourage Oppressed Nations.** lamp set upon a hill to guide and encourage the nations of the earth that are now struggling for independence. In spite of the prejudices, hatred and persecution which the Jews as a race have suffered in all ages, that race has been a positive help and benefit to the peoples and governments that persecuted them.

"The Jews as a people are wise, conservative, patriotic **In Hearty Accord with Zionism.** and provident. I am, therefore, in most hearty accord with the sentiment expressed by Mr. Balfour and I trust that the Zionist movement may effectuate in the gratification of the aspirations of the brave men and women who have conceived and are pushing forward this great enterprise.

"I thank you for the opportunity to express my views on the subject." (Signed) "Jas. K. Vardaman."

By Senator John Sharp Williams,
Of Mississippi.

Epoch in
History of
Civilization.

"I am in absolute sympathy with the 'Jewry,' with the Zionists, and with the British Government, in the announcement of its policy in Palestine. I think it all constitutes an epoch in the history of the 'Chosen Race,' and, still more than that, it constitutes an epoch *in the history of civilization* and the right of nationalities to self-determination."

(Signed)   "JOHN SHARP WILLIAMS."

By Senator James A. Reed,
Of Missouri.

Jewish Re-
establish-
ment to
Benefit
Humanity.

"I believe it would make for the peace of the world and the welfare of humanity if a great nation composed of Jewish people would be established where the Jewish race so long maintained the highest type of civilization then known to the world. The influence of such a nation might do much toward regenerating what may almost be called a lost continent in Asia."

(Signed)   "JAS. A. REED."

By Senator Xenophon P. Wilfley,
Of Missouri.

"In regard to the Jewish land in Palestine and the Declarations of England, France, and Italy with reference thereto, it seems to me to open up a new phase on the Jewish question. It seems to me as though Palestine should be made a national center or a national home for the Jewish people. They have always stood for right, justice and religion. I feel confident that they will continue to stand for the same ideals in their Homeland.

"The Jewish people have been misunderstood so often that I believe the time has come to set them aright by making them the guardians of Palestine without in any way prejudicing the non-Jewish people who may live there. I have no doubt the rights of these people would be religiously observed by the Zionists. Re-establishment of a Jewish Homeland in Palestine would tend to settle many vexing problems and it seems to me the natural and logical thing to do."

(Signed)   "XENOPHON P. WILFLEY."

By Senator Henry L. Myers,
Of Montana.

"I approve of the British Declaration in favor of a Jewish Homeland in Palestine. I do so because I believe it right and just, based on sound reasons and for the benefit of a people who have done a great deal for the world.

"Regarding Zionism generally, it is, of course, entirely of concern to the Jews, and I believe in extending them every legitimate facility in realizing it."

(Signed)   "H. L. MYERS."

By Senator Gilbert M. Hitchcock,
Of Nebraska.

Settle Vexed
Jewish
Question.

"The British Declaration in favor of a Jewish State in the Holy Land seems to me a logical and generous statement of the British position. It affords to the Jewish people an opportunity of settling one of the vexed Jewish questions, and guarantees them protection in their cherished desire to return to Palestine. I doubt whether many American Jews will ever avail themselves of the offer, because their opportunities are better in the United States than they would be in Palestine or anywhere else that I know of. For purely sentimental reasons, Jews who have fought the battle of life and desire to close their days in a reconstructed Holy Land may be induced to go even from America, but for the most part it will only be the oppressed Jews of countries where their lot is a hard one that will join in the Zionist movement to any great extent.

Duty of
American
Jews to
Help.

Fortunate Jews of America can help them and ought to. The idea of Zionism is a big one and appeals to the imagination. I have no idea that it will be abandoned until it has been fairly tried."

(Signed)   "G. M. HITCHCOCK."

By Senator Key Pittman,
Of Nevada.

Sympathetic
and Will
Assist.

"I am in thorough accord with the deep and sympathetic interest of the President of the United States in the welfare of the Jewish nation as expressed in his letter on Zionism; and as a member of the United States Senate, I will give every effort to put into effect the plan now suggested on this question or any other plan that may be formulated by the President."

(Signed)   "KEY PITTMAN."

By Senator Irving W. Drew,
Of New Hampshire.

"I agree very fully with the statements made by Senator Lodge and others.* I think there ought to be a Jewish Home in Palestine, in accordance with the official Declaration of President Wilson and our Allies."

Will Support Jewish Home.

(Signed) "IRVING W. DREW."

By Senator Joseph S. Frelinghuysen,
Of New Jersey.

"I am sorry that I have not had an opportunity to give the question of Zionism very much study and attention. Of course I could not help becoming acquainted with it to some degree, especially in the last year or so when it has gained such prominence in non-Jewish circles.

"I entirely approve the announcement of Secretary Balfour, and gladly support the present British policy on this question, or any policy it may adopt in the near future, in conjunction with our own country, and the other nations of the earth, now in alliance with us; such policy to be in fulfillment of the requirements of international diplomacy and in compliance with the aspirations of the Jewish race.

Approves Balfour Announcement.

"From what I have said above you can easily see that I would be heartily in favor of a resolution which would embody the sentiments that I have just expressed. I should be very pleased to feel that my aid would prove beneficial to the very worthy cause which the Jews have in view."

Favors Congress Resolution.

(Signed) "J. S. FRELINGHUYSEN."

---

* See statement by Senator Lodge, page 43.

By Senator Albert B. Fall,
Of New Mexico.

"I am cordially in sympathy with the British Declaration with reference to Palestine. Of course, this statement applies equally to the declarations of France and Italy.

Favors Action by United States.

"I would favor action by the United States Government along lines of the other declarations referred to, either at present, or at any time in the future.

Will Support Resolution by Congress.

"I will favor the adoption of proper resolutions by Congress in favor of the establishment of a Jewish National center in Palestine.

"I am in sympathy with any action which the Jewish people desire to take, or have taken, to establish a national home in Palestine.

To Assist Palestine Establishment.

"I may say frankly that I regard the great majority of Jews in the United States as loyal American citizens. I expect to see a great majority remain American citizens. To such of the Jews as may desire to establish actual residence in Palestine, I am willing to extend any assistance possible.

Maintain Religious Freedom in Diaspora.

"With respect to the Jews who I believe will continue to reside in the United States, I, of course, recognize not only their right, but the propriety of their action in maintaining their religious beliefs and observances, as the same right is recognized to all other people or members of all other denominations or sects. Such maintenance of religious beliefs or observances of same will never, of course, conflict with the patriotic duty of American citizens."

(Signed)   "ALBERT B. FALL."

By Senator William M. Calder,
Of New York.

"Yes, I have heard of the British Declaration and would give it my utmost support, especially since it has been adopted practically by all of our Allies. To me it is a very simple proposition—if the Jews want a homeland in Palestine, and if it is possible to accomplish that end, as all indications seem to warrant, why not let them have it? More than that: Why not aid them in this sincere and just demand or desire?

"Let me say to you that I do not, of course, consider this Zionist restoration to be of the same character as the Belgian restoration. It is somewhat difficult for the casual observer to think of the Jews *now* as a nation, in the same sense as we think of the Belgians. The Jews are now lacking certain factors that go to make up a nation and national life, and if I understand it correctly, this is the reason for Zionism, with some people. Certainly this is why I would support the Declaration for the Jewish homeland as proclaimed by our Allies. The realization of this promise would make the national life of the Jews complete.

"I appreciate that at the present moment the Jews form only a minority of the Palestine population, but I know that these Jews have built up the colonies of the Holy Land and form the *weightier* part of the inhabitants, in many respects. I, for one, am ready to leave the restoration and upbuilding of Palestine to Jewish brains and energy. It would be only a short duration of time, before the Jews would form the majority of the population in the Holy Land, from every viewpoint. Your people may depend upon my aid toward causing the realization of the hope for Jewish restoration whenever the opportunity will be offered to me."

(Signed)   "WILLIAM M. CALDER."

By Senator James W. Wadsworth, Jr.,
Of New York.

Project Deserves Universal Support.

"It appears to me that from every viewpoint the reestablishment of the Jewish Homeland in Palestine is certainly a very worthy project which should have the support of every nation and individual no matter what their economic, political, social, or religious creed be. I am certainly glad of the fact that Great Britain, one of the great democratic powers of the world, came out for this Zionist principle at the most opportune time. I should have been even more glad if our own country had been the first to declare itself for the principles as laid down by the Balfour statement. However, due to certain relative international complications, as you can easily understand, America could not have proclaimed officially its support of the Jewish Home Land in Palestine, at the time when Great Britain deemed it proper to do so. But this should not deter any one in this country from giving his support to this noble and lofty ideal of your people.

Zionist Realization Mere Justice.

"It is merely a case of common and accepted justice on the part of all of us to see that this project of the reestablishment of your glory of old be realized to its fullest extent and at the earliest possible moment. The Jewish nation ought to be protected in its newly-planned homeland in every possible way, its individual members scattered all over the world are bound to gain absolute equality and freedom in every land where they may be found. It certainly is logical to assume that this very establishment of your new national life and government will aid your brethren to a great degree in their land.

Accords with Wilson's Principles.

"When I think of the destiny to be decided at the end of this war, of the various small nationalities, a destiny which we hope will be decided according to their own wishes and aspirations, I cannot for one moment exclude the Hebrews from that worthy group of smaller nations that have given their all in this war along with the other powers of the world. President Wilson's principles of democracy will be the savior of these nationalities among whom your people play a very prominent part. I, on my part, will do everything in my power to aid this cause in my own way whenever I shall be called upon to do so. Your cause is the cause of all humanity."

(Signed)   "J. W. WADSWORTH, JR."

54

By Senator Lee Slater Overman,
Of North Carolina.

"I would be very glad to see Palestine restored to the Jews, its original owners, in accordance with the strong yearnings of so many Jews and non-Jews. I see every possible reason to give my approval and support to the British Declaration. I hope that this Declaration will be realized and come true as soon as this Great War is over.

Wishes Palestine Restored to Jews.

"The formation of a Jewish Republic, in the Holy Land, populated by those of your brethren who would choose to make it their home, will, to my mind, be another strong link in the chain of small nations, who have a right—and a duty—to determine their own fate and future, without any foreign interference. The United States would indeed welcome this just step.

Jewish Duty to Determine Future.

"Why am I so strongly for the British Declaration and for the Palestine Jewish Restoration? Let me mention one reason. I favor it because, as I gather from various sources, very many Jews desire it. This is sufficient ground for me, and it ought to be for every non-biased thinking man. I hardly need to add that the Jewish State in Palestine would prosper and prove beneficial even to those living beyond its territorial limits.

State Will Benefit All Jews.

"This, I deem, is the opinion of the citizens of this country, of every creed and denomination. The patriotism of the American Jews cannot be questioned in the remotest degree, because of their Zionistic tendencies, any more than the loyalty of the Belgians here can be questioned because of their hope for the restoration of their land to its rightful owners."

Zionism and Patriotism Compatible.

(Signed) "LEE S. OVERMAN."

By Senator Porter J. McCumber,
Of North Dakota.

Is Pledged by Allies.

"In the midst of this world carnage, a great Nation, while bearing the brunt of that most desperate conflict of the ages, has written in letters of fire across the black clouds of battle that Israel shall be returned to her ancient heritage. This purpose is now included among the many noble purposes to which the Allies striving in concert are pledged. So far it is a declaration of purpose only. Its consummation depends upon the sword of the Allies, and the complete victory of those nations pledged to destroy militarism and to assure the sacred rights of all peoples. The price of Achievement must be paid for with the blood of many hundreds of thousands of our bravest and best.

Christian World Approves.

"The Christian world joins the Jewish in hearty laudation and earnest approval of this declaration.

"The eyes of Israel, dimmed by sorrow and clouded by persecution, have ever seen the vision of the reconstructed Temple and the re-established glory of the Holy City.

"The history of Palestine, the birthplace of enlightenment, and of Jerusalem, the city of ancient literature, poetry, and philosophy, are enshrined in the hearts of both Jew and Christian the world over. From this fountain head Israel has drawn her undying inspiration and Christendom its religion of love and mercy.

Delayed Justice Assured— Zionism a Reality.

"Let us, therefore, join our hearts in fervent hope and heroic resolution that all the sacrifices we have made, all we must make in the future to consummate this purpose shall not have been made in vain; and that the prayers of the Jewish people which have ascended to Heaven through twenty centuries may now be answered, and Justice, long delayed, be now assured; that after two thousand years of banishment, the sons of this virile, historic race may regather from every corner of the earth and their hearts respond in truth as well as in sentiment to the words, 'This is my own, my native land,' and that in their just joy and pride they may ever remember the great cause and the great nations of the earth which, joined together for human rights and world justice, have made the dream of Zionism a mighty reality.

"France and Italy have publicly approved the declaration of the British Government favoring the establishment in Palestine of a National Home for the Jewish people. The people of the United States, being heartily in accord, Congress through proper resolution should give to it the force of National purpose." *United States Should Accord National Support.*

(Signed) "PORTER J. MCCUMBER."

By Senator F. M. Simmons,
Of North Carolina.

"I am in hearty accord with the purpose of our Allies, France, England, and Italy, as expressed in the official declarations of these countries with respect to the Zionist question. *In Accord with Zionism.*

"I am led to this conclusion because of an earnest desire to see the Holy Places taken forever from Turkish control. This being accomplished, it seems to me that all Americans will agree that the Jews are the natural guardians of these places. Obedience to the laws of all lands by the Jews should disabuse the minds of the doubtful with respect to the Jews carrying out any agreement as to the rights of non-Jewish peoples. *Jews Natural Guardians of Palestine.*

"I should be glad to see Congress adopt an appropriate resolution with regard to this matter." *Favors Congressional Resolution.*

(Signed) "F. M. SIMMONS."

By Senator Thomas P. Gore,
Of Oklahoma.

Ever a
Forceful
Appeal.

"From my youth up, the Zionist movement appealed with peculiar force to my imagination. An appeal to this sort as you will readily appreciate has a stronger hold upon the youthful imagination than upon the more mature judgment. I will make my meaning clearer as I proceed. If anyone should charge that my state of mind towards Turkey is one of prejudice, I could with good conscience plead 'not guilty.' Turkey has been the scourge of modern civilization. She has almost earned the reputation of being an outlaw among the nations. The tyranny and the cruelty which she has perpetrated upon weaker people has forfeited every claim, I will not say of justice but certainly to generosity in judging of her history and her policies.

"It is with me a deep seated and enduring hope that Palestine may be permanently rescued from the toils of this ruthless and blighting despotism. It is my earnest hope that the independence and the integrity of Palestine may be securely established and guaranteed as one of the beneficent results of this war. It is my hope that both the substance and the shadow of tyranny shall be forever banished from this ancient and historic land. It is my hope that all the Jews who inhabit the hills and vales of Palestine may be inviolably safeguarded in the enjoyment of life, liberty, and property, and in the pursuit of happiness. It is my hope that the gates not only of Jerusalem but of Palestine itself shall stand ajar and above them shall be written welcome to all the descendants of Abraham, Isaac, and Jacob. It is my hope that the footsore and heartsore Jews from every clime, victims of an immemorial oppression and persecution may be vouchsafed the privilege and the right to return to the land of their fathers and work out their own destiny in their own way. It is my hope that the humblest Jew in the most oppressed land shall be permitted to find in Palestine, not an asylum, not a house of refuge, but a home where all the blessings of civilized life shall be his inviolable inheritance and where none shall come to molest or to make him afraid.

Palestine
Not Asylum
but Home
for Jews.

58

"I reserve any opinion as to the wisdom of any con- **No Compul-**
certed movement, campaign, or crusade to induce the **sion on**
Israelites to return to the land of Israel. Certainly no **Jews.**
compulsion legal or moral should be exerted first to
make exiles of the Jews and then to make them unwilling citizens of Palestine. The considerations which induce me to make these observations are so numerous and
so obvious as to make discussion entirely superfluous."

(Signed)   "T. P. GORE."

By Senator Robert L. Owen,
Of Oklahoma.

"I have thought it would be well to establish in Pa- **State to**
lestine a distinct Jewish state where the genius of that **Preserve**
race for order and government might be offered to the **Jewish**
world, and moreover, where the historical character of **Character.**
the Hebrew race might be kept alive and presented as a
living entity to the world.

"This does not, in my judgment, minimize the value **Jews of**
of the members of the Hebrew race in their capacities **Service**
as citizens of other nations. I should be glad to see the **Throughout**
race, both as a distinct self-governing nation, and as **World.**
individuals given every possible opportunity to serve the
world."   (Signed)   "ROBERT L. OWEN."

By Senator George E. Chamberlain,
Of Oregon.

"The attitude of England, France and Italy on the **Favors**
Zionist question meets with my approval, because it pro- **United**
vides for the establishment of a home at the very cradle **States**
of a race, and where its most remarkable history was **Action.**
made and recorded. I do not see why the United States
should not officially make a declaration in line with that
of the Honorable Arthur J. Balfour, Secretary of State
for Foreign Affairs; and Congress too might with propriety adopt a resolution along the same line. Such a
course will give aid to the movement of the Jewish people
to establish a National Home in Palestine and inspirit
them in what seems to me to be a most laudable undertaking."   (Signed)   "GEO. E. CHAMBERLAIN."

59

By Senator Charles L. McNary,
Of Oregon.

Public Recognition of Jewish Nationality.

"The official pronouncements of our Allies in favor of the Zionist program marks a new epoch in the history of the Jews. These Declarations give formal public recognition that Israel as a nation is still alive and will persist. This was necessary for the reason that some few people were skeptical as to the national entity of the Jews. All doubt as to this phase being totally dispelled now, it remains for those of the Jewish people who will settle in their old—but new—home, to make Palestine, a veritable Jewish State as is looked for by their brethren all over.

Zionist Realization is Ideal— Beneficial to All.

"Palestine is the connecting link between Europe and Asia. The Jews, originally hailing from Asia, but who have become Europeans in their diaspora extending for two thousand years, may now also serve as a link between the people of these two great continents. It is, thus, a piece of good fortune that the Jews should become the governing people of Palestine. This, added to the fact, that the Holy Land is their historic home, the land of their dreams, and ambitions, makes the realization of Zionism at this time almost ideal. Europe may expect great results and much benefit from this promised State of Judea, and the Allied Governments will not be the losers in helping Israel in this accomplishment.

"I wish to send through you my greetings and good wishes to the Jewish State, and hope, as I am confident, that it will prosper and grow as in the days of old."

(Signed)   "CHARLES L. MCNARY."

60

By Senator Boies Penrose,
Of Pennsylvania.

"I am entirely in sympathy with the views of which Zionism is the expression.

For Complete Endorsement by United States.

"I believe that the Government of the United States should take action in line with the British declaration on the Zionist question. Palestine and the Holy Places of both the Christian and Jewish religions should be forever removed from Turkish control. I have had for many years full opportunity to become familiar with and to appreciate the valued contributions of the Jewish people to our American institutions and I am ready at all times cordially to meet their aspirations.

"I am in full sympathy with the efforts of the Jewish people to establish a national home in Palestine, and recognize the significance of such a proposition after the struggle through centuries."

Significance of Zionism.

(Signed) "BOIES PENROSE."

By Senator Le Baron B. Colt,
Of Rhode Island.

"I am very glad to give expression to my views on this subject.

"I fully approve of the Honorable Arthur J. Balfour's declaration in favor of the establishment in Palestine of a National Home for the Jewish people, for I entertain the highest regard and respect for them.

Approves Balfour Declaration.

"I feel that suitable action might well be taken by our Government at the proper time along the line of the declaration by the British Government in support of this National Jewish Home plan, and should an appropriate resolution be offered I will certainly give the matter very careful attention and consideration in the light of my high regard for the Jewish people. Personally I cannot too highly commend their attitude in inaugurating this movement, for I believe that the establishment of such a Home will tend to unify and crystallize the Jewish national spirit and yet at the same time will not in any degree detract from that loyalty to America and American institutions so characteristic of the Jewish people."

Crystallizes National Spirit.

(Signed) "LE BARON B. COLT."

By Senator Christie Benet,
Of South Carolina.

Let United States Effect Realization.

"I approve of the official Declarations of England, France and Italy on the Zionist question and believe the time has now come for vigorous action on the part of the United States not only to set its approval on the Declaration but to put the terms of that declaration into effect as soon as possible. I see no reason why Congress would not act promptly on the matter, and believe that such action would tend to hearten the Jews all over the world.

For Action by Congress.

"Such being my belief I would favor the adoption of a proper Resolution by Congress in favor of the establishment in Palestine of a Jewish National Center. A race without a home is a tragedy and I believe that the time is now here when the Jews can have a home and that home should be Palestine."

(Signed)   "CHRISTIE BENET."

By Senator Kenneth D. McKellar,
Of Tennessee.

For Congressional Resolution.

"I take pleasure in saying that I approve of the statement of Mr. Arthur J. Balfour of date November 2nd, 1917, favoring the establishment in Palestine of a national home for the Jewish people. I hope that the United States Government, by appropriate resolution, will favor the establishment in Palestine of a Jewish National Center.

Jewish Homeland Desirable.

"At the present the Jews have taken leading places in all the countries of the world and yet they have no independent nationality. The history of this remarkable race, its sacred and profound literature, its social cohesiveness, its worth and power, all make it peculiarly desirable that it should have a distinct national home.

Most Appropriate Time.

"There was never a better time to re-establish this home in Palestine than at the present time and I trust that in the settlements which must come after the war it will be so arranged that a Jewish center shall be established in this historic land of the Jews."

(Signed)   "KENNETH D. McKELLAR."

By Senator Thomas Sterling,
Of South Dakota.

"I heartily approve the declaration of the British Government, made through Mr. Balfour, and endorsed by the Governments of France and Italy, in favor of the establishment of a National Home in Palestine for the Jewish people. I favor this declaration because of the place the Jewish people have in the civilization of the world and because it was in Palestine that the Jewish ideals of religion, of society and of government were brought into their most perfect realization. *National Restoration Will Further Civilization.*

"While the Jewish people, by their intermingling with other nationalities and their manifest adaptability to new conditions, have ceased to be regarded as the peculiar and exclusive people they once were, still, through all the changes and vicissitudes of the centuries, they seem to have preserved many of the noblest traditions and ideals of their race. *Jews Preserve Ideals of Race.*

"I am confident that the establishment of the National Home in Palestine, while recognizing fully the civil and religious rights of non-Jewish communities there, will have a wholesome, humanizing and civilizing effect upon the people of other communities and races in that region. *Humanizing Effect of Jewish State.*

"I am, therefore, now inclined to look with favor upon the adoption of an appropriate resolution by Congress in favor of the establishment in Palestine of a Jewish National Centre." *Favors Resolution.*

(Signed) "THOMAS STERLING."

By Senator Charles A. Culberson,
Of Texas.

"I feel a very deep interest in the subject of the establishment of a Jewish Homeland in Palestine in accordance with the British, French and Italian declarations, and will be glad to render any assistance in my power toward the achievement of this object." *Will Assist.*

(Signed) "C. A. CULBERSON."

By Senator Morris Sheppard,
Of Texas.

In Hearty Sympathy.

"With the efforts of those of the Jewish people who desire to re-establish the Jewish Republic in Palestine, I am in hearty sympathy.

Heritage of Ancient State.

"Faith in the God of the spirit and the idea of spiritual and political brotherhood which flowered from that faith, enabled the Jewish people in the early stages of history to erect the world's first self-governing commonwealth, a commonwealth embodying the fundamentals of civilization, culture, law, order, and equality. This commonwealth was finally destroyed by the Roman despotism which engulfed the world. The germ of human liberty which had been so thoroughly developed by the Jewish nation outlived the Roman Empire, the incursions and rule of the barbarians, medieval ignorance, superstition and violence, and today finds rich fruition in the lands that are resisting the attempt of a modern Caesar and a modern Rome to set up a universal tyranny.

Let Jerusalem Rise!

"The old Caesar destroyed the Jewish nation. The imperial dreams of the new Caesar, to wit: the Hohenzollerns, the Hapsburgs and the Mohammeds, are soon to be destroyed by the modern peoples in whom the liberty of Israel lives again. When Jerusalem fell, the old Rome continued to rise. Today, eighteen and a half centuries later, as Berlin, the modern Rome, totters to its fall, let Jerusalem rise! Such a spectacle would vastly aid in perpetuating the ideal of human liberty. It would thrill and inspire the world. It would epitomize history. It would glorify equality, and would be a lasting and dramatic tribute to the deathlessness of democracy.

Duty of United States to Act.

"I approve the declarations of England, France and Italy on the subject of a new Zion in Palestine. I think the United States should encourage the movement, and that Congress should adopt an appropriate resolution."

(Signed)   "MORRIS SHEPPARD."

By Senator William H. King,
Of Utah.

"The statement by Hon. Arthur J. Balfour, Secretary of State for Foreign Affairs, in the present British Ministry, is in my opinion, the statement of a very desirable and proper policy to be pursued with reference to the constitution of a free government for Palestine. I note that the views of Mr. Balfour are endorsed by the official representatives of the French Government and the Italian Government. Balfour Statement Proper Policy.

"Certainly all friends of liberty and progress in the world would be gratified to see the national aspirations of the Jews and the re-establishment of their ancient home in Palestine realized and accomplished. It need not to be said that the Government of the United States in view of its traditional policy for the promotion and protection of republican institutions, and particularly on the American continent as embodied in the Monroe doctrine, could do other than look with favor and approval upon the establishment of a free state in Palestine and the integration of the national aspirations, culture, and liberties of the Jewish people." United States Government Favors Jewish National Aspirations.

"It may not be necessary or opportune at this time for Congress to make a declaration upon this subject. The views and attitude of our Government cannot in any event be other than as indicated above. It may not, however, be wise to interfere with the development of this movement by a Congressional declaration, before there is a more perfect formulation of plans for the accomplishment of this project, which the liberal governments that are waging this war for liberty and the rights of nations will heartily approve and support." Congress Action Perhaps Inopportune.

(Signed)   "WILLIAM H. KING."

By Senator Reed Smoot,
Of Utah.

Re-estab-
lishment to
be Realized.

"The British Declaration for Zionism came as a logical consequence in the aims of our Allies for re-establishment of small nationalities in their proper sphere. Not only do I believe in the Jewish homeland in Palestine, but I am certain and confident that it will come about as foretold by prophets of old and that the present World War will hasten the day of its consummation. We, on our part, will do our share in helping the Jewish people to realize their national aspirations that they have had for many centuries and especially within recent years.

American
Jews and
Christians
Should Aid.

"Let me say to you that I emphasize this not only as a good American, but also as a good Christian. I see every reason for the American Jews to give this movement their entire support. It is their duty as well as the duty of every good American. Aside from the international, economic, social and religious aspect, I consider it very fascinating and inspiring. I should consider it a pleasure to aid in my own way in the realization of the dream of the Jewish people for the last two thousand years."

(Signed) "Reed Smoot."

By Senator W. P. Dillingham,
Of Vermont.

Favors
Center for
Jewish
Thought.

"If I understand aright the Declarations of England, France and Italy on the Zionist question I approve them.

"It would seem to be especially fitting that there be established in Palestine a real center of Jewish national thought. If the scheme can be wrought out and developed along reasonable lines and under conditions that will permit liberty of thought and action among all classes and in such a way as to attract from all parts of the world men of the Hebrew faith, it would be most desirable.

"The civilization of the present century ought to make possible the realization of such a hope without opposition from those of other faiths."

(Signed) "W. P. Dillingham."

66

By Senator Miles Poindexter,
Of Washington.

"The occupation of Palestine by the British forces and the Declaration on November 2, 1917, by the British Minister of Foreign Affairs, favoring and encouraging the establishment of a Jewish community of immigrants of that race from all portions of the world in Palestine, is one of the most valuable developments of the great world war. I trust that it is illustrative of many other refreshing and strengthening readjustments which will be arranged when peace is made.

> *One of Great War Readjustments.*

"The great opportunity thus offered will be a healing balm to the hearts of hundreds, of thousands, and perhaps millions, of scattered Hebrews in all parts of the world. Many of them have had this great ideal before their eyes in hope and imagination for many years, and its consummation will seem like compensation, in part, for the sufferings and tribulations and wanderings through long ages and generations of the race. While, perhaps, the return to Palestine may not appeal to all Jews, to many, and especially to those who have preserved in their full vigor the Jewish national traditions —it will be a happy and consecrated event.

> *Part Compensation for Sufferings.*

"The history of the Jewish race is the best illustration of the predominance of ideas. It never ruled over a great country, nor possessed, as compared with other civilizations, valuable natural resources; and yet the history of its development, its literature, religion, and laws, and even the personal incidents and genealogies of its members and rulers, are parts of the household life and culture of the most powerful ruling race of the world.

> *Race Illustrates Predominance of Ideas.*

"To be re-established in the very places and origins of their ancient power, and to occupy again the very seats from which were spoken those mighty words which have ruled mankind, must be, to many Jews, the deepest satisfaction and happiness. This re-establishment of their people, or a portion of them, in a self-governing community under the protection of a great free empire, will add a new source of strength and inspiration to the world. It will be the regeneration in a sense of the race, benefitting mankind by adding to the communities of peoples another one, where happiness, freedom, and opportunity prevail.   67

> *Will Benefit Race and Mankind.*

Zionist
Movement
Heartily
Approved.

"Having expelled the Turkish legions, the British have dispelled tyranny, and brought protection of life and property, freedom of worship, and work, to Palestine; and this may be an omen of the material and spiritual improvement of that land and of those who will, under these happy auspices, come to occupy it, if the plan proposed is carried out. It has my hearty approval and co-operation." (Signed) "MILES POINDEXTER."

By Senator Wesley L. Jones,
Of Washington.

Admires
Devotion to
Palestine.

"I sympathize most sincerely with the hopes and aspirations of the Jewish people, and admire greatly their steadfast devotion to the land of their birth.

For Self-
Determina-
tion.

"I can see no objection to the Declaration made by the British Government, but I do not know enough about the real objects and purposes sought by your organization to feel qualified to express a fixed opinion upon them, nor am I prepared to say what action, if any, the nation or Congress should take. I conceive this enterprise to be something which must be worked out largely, if not entirely, by your people.

For Action
by Executive
or Congress.

"No objection to a resolution by Congress, or a declaration on the part of our Government, occurs to me now, but with the limited knowledge which I have of your project, it would be unwise and presumptuous for me to say what Congress or the nation should or should not do in regard to it. I may say that I have some very positive ideas as to what the attitude of all those claiming to be American citizens should be towards other countries or sovereignties. Those who have preserved

No Weak-
ening of
Allegiance.

their nationality and desire to maintain their allegiance to their native land, should be prompted to do so; but those who have become citizens of this country, either by birth or adoption, should have no divided allegiance. This is the time for every American citizen to be an American citizen, and I do not desire to do anything by suggestion or otherwise to weaken the allegiance of any of our citizens, and especially those who have become such by adoption." (Signed) "W. L. JONES."

By Senator Howard Sutherland,
Of West Virginia.

"I am glad to give my approval to the pronounce- **Matter of Justice.**
ments of the Allies indorsing Zionism, for the reason
that I believe it a matter of international justice that the
Jewish people, after a lapse of these years, may have an
opportunity to establish a National Home in Palestine,
where they may live in peace and contentment and free
from race prejudices or hatreds.

"I see no reason why the U. S. Government should **Would Support a**
not make a similar declaration to that already made by **Resolution**
England, France and Italy; and if such resolution is **of Congress.**
brought before Congress for adoption I shall be glad to
favor it.

"I believe that this effort of the Jewish people to **Wishing Success.**
establish a National Home in Palestine may result finally
in giving the Jewish people a permanent home upon soil
hallowed by many sacred memories, and I wish them all
success in this most commendable enterprise."

(Signed)   "HOWARD SUTHERLAND."

By Senator Irvine L. Lenroot,
Of Wisconsin.

"I am in hearty accord with the efforts of the Jewish **Favors**
people to establish a National Home in Palestine, with- **Palestine**
out prejudice to the civil and religious rights of non- **Homeland.**
Jewish communities there."

(Signed)   "I. L. LENROOT."

By Senator John B. Kendrick,
Of Wyoming.

General Approbation of American People.

"The aspiration of the Jewish people for the establishment in Palestine of a national home will, I am sure, meet with the general sympathy and approbation of the people of the United States, particularly at this time when the whole civilized world is united in a concentrated effort to secure the principle of self determination for all races.

Erect State in Cradle of Race.

"There is no doubt now that Palestine, having been freed from the domination of the Turks, will never be restored to that alien rule. I can see no reason why, in the place of the government which has been deposed, the nations of the world should not unite to erect a Jewish State in the cradle of the ancient race which has survived through the centuries all manner of oppression."

(Signed)   "JOHN B. KENDRICK."

By Senator Francis E. Warren,
Of Wyoming.

Favors Self-Determination of Nationalities.

"Quoting from your letter that: 'In view of President Wilson's utterances in favor of the rights of all similar nationalities, which are to be given the opportunity of determining their own futures, it is of the utmost interest to the Jewish people of the United States to be informed of the opinion of the members of the United States Senate and of the House of Representatives on this important question' I beg to concur in President Wilson's remarks favoring the solution of this matter."

(Signed)   "F. E. WARREN."

70

Statements of
Representatives*

*Including delegates from territorial possessions of the United States

By Representative William B. Bankhead,
Of Alabama.

"I am unequivocally in favor of the return of Judea to the Jews not merely as an act of abstract justice and not for the mere reason that the international situation just now seems to point to the expediency of such a State. but more because of the contribution to the science of government a new Jewish State will mean. Restoration Will Benefit World.

"From the days of the Bible, to the present era, the Jews have been formidable in the field of ethics. They were constantly teaching morals to the other nations and do that now. For two thousand years they were deprived of the opportunity, however, to exemplify these teachings. Government is essentially the practice of a standard of ethics between man and his fellow man. By the establishment of a Jewish State, the opportunity will be furnished for providing such a model of government to the other nations that shall inspire emulation by the rest of the world. Model State of Jews.

"Furthermore, it may be expected that the world's art and culture will be enriched by such contributions in those fields as will be made by a Jewish State. Jews have heretofore made notable achievements in these lines but not as Jews. They were Frenchmen or Englishmen or Russians, of the Jewish faith, but not Jews. There is a marked distinction between the two. In Palestine Jewish talent and ability will unfold itself and be given the opportunity of self expression. It will mean a great gain to the world culture and progress. True Jewish Culture to Be Realized.

"I have no doubt that these considerations played a great part in the decisions of the allied governments in taking their official steps in favor of a Jewish Homeland in Palestine in accordance with the Zionist principles. It will be very gratifying to me to have an opportunity to help the accomplishment of this movement in such a manner as may be at my disposal at the proper time. The Jews of the world may depend upon my assistance." Will Aid Movement.

(Signed)   "WM. B. BANKHEAD."

By Representative John L. Burnett,
Of Alabama.

In Accord with Declaration. "I am perfectly in accord with every word of the so-called British Declaration for the establishment in Palestine of a National Home for the Jewish people. As stated by Secretary Balfour, it is clearly understood that nothing should be done which may prejudice the civil and religious rights of non-Jewish communities in Palestine or the rights and political status enjoyed by Jews in any other country. To this end I shall give my utmost support, if necessary, in every possible way.

Zionism Ennobling Movement. "Zionism, therefore, as it is practically expressed in this Declaration has my sympathy and is promised my assistance. This conclusion I have reached after examining the question to some degree, and after discussing it with you and others on several occasions. I think the cause of Zionism and the movement for a Jewish Nationalism is a very worthy and ennobling one, one that reminds us of the great contributions that the Jews have given to the world and the lofty mission that Israel has had in its long historic past.

Will not Prejudice Jewish Rights Elsewhere. "Let me say, furthermore, that Zionism and the kind of Jewish Nationalism that I would support is the one that would not force any Jew, in those countries where he has become a full citizen and perfectly acclimatized, to leave such country and join the new land of Zion. Nor do I believe this new country should exclude from its midst any Jews who may come there from the countries where they have been oppressed and discriminated against. I thus fully realize the great ideal of the movement.

Favors Action by United States. "It is my opinion that the United States should take steps similar to the ones taken by the other allied governments regarding the problem of Zionism. Whether this should be in a form of a declaration by the Executive department or by a proper resolution in Congress is of little moment to me. Either of the two methods would get my approval. It is a matter for the Jews themselves to decide which one to consider best."

(Signed) "JOHN L. BURNETT."

By Representative Oscar L. Gray,
Of Alabama.

"I heartily approve of the Declarations of England, A Harbinger
France and Italy on the Zionist question. My reasons of Better
for favoring these Declarations are based on a deep Things.
sympathy for the race which has, for many centuries,
been without a National Home; and from a sense of
justice to a people who have given to the world, literature and ideals which have been the source of inspiration
to countless numbers of men and women. It is to the
Jewish race that we owe the history of the human family
as given in the Old Testament; it is to the Jews that we
must give honor for such men as Moses, David, and the
prophets, who have given to us the Moral Law and the
faith inspiring Psalms, with their comfort and confident
praise. I believe that the establishment in Palestine of a
National Home for the Jewish people would mean a
great constructive and progressive movement for these
people, whose faith has remained undimmed throughout
the years of their tribulations. It would mean a harbinger of better things for all mankind, for would it
not mean that the time for the fulfillment of the
prophesy was at hand, when Israel should be gathered
from the four corners of the earth, and be again established in Jerusalem, the City of David, around which
there still clings the spiritual incense of religious inspiration: when the dawn of a new day will be seen
from the mountains, heralding the brotherhood of man,
and the establishment of the Kingdom of God.

"I assuredly favor action by the United States in line For
with the British Declaration, now or in the near future, Action by
and as stated, it being clearly understood, that nothing Government.
shall be done which may prejudice the civil rights of
non-Jewish communities in Palestine, or the rights and
political status enjoyed by Jews in any other country.

"Should this question, as before stated, come before Would
Congress, in the form of an appropriate resolution, I Support
would favor its adoption, for the establishment in Pales- Congress
time of a Jewish National Centre. Resolution.

75

Deserves
Support of
Liberty
Lovers.

"My views in general in regard to this effort are, as before stated, that it is a very worthy one, and deserves the support of all liberty loving people who desire to hold together in unity and love. I am glad for this opportunity to express my views on this subject, and will certainly co-operate in any movement that will help the Jewish People to establish a National Centre in Palestine, their original home."

(Signed) "Oscar L. Gray."

By Representative Fred L. Blackmon, Of Alabama.

Friendly but
Withholds
Opinion.

"I am a staunch friend of the Jewish people and will do anything I can consistently to help them, but I would not declare my position on any question until it is up to me for decision."

(Signed) "Fred L. Blackmon."

By Representative S. Hubert Dent, Of Alabama.

For Jewish
Homeland
in Palestine.

"I am heartily in favor of the establishment in Palestine of a home for the Jewish people subject to the condition that nothing be done which would in any way interfere with the religious and civil rights of non-Jewish people."

(Signed) "S. H. Dent, Jr."

By Representative J. Thomas Heflin, Of Alabama.

Re-estab-
lishment
is Fine
Suggestion.

"I am in hearty sympathy with any plan that will better the condition of the Jews in the old World, and the suggestion of establishing a Jewish Homeland in Palestine for Jews of every country, which has been endorsed by the President, I think, is a fine suggestion."

(Signed) "J. Thos. Heflin."

By Representative William B. Oliver,
Of Alabama.

"I feel a keen interest and sympathy in the move- Keenly In-
ment to found a Jewish Homeland in Palestine." terested in
Movement.

(Signed)   "W. B. OLIVER."

By Representative Thaddeus H. Caraway,
Of Arkansas.

"I am in full accord with the Balfour Declaration For Dec-
favoring a Jewish Homeland in Palestine. laration.

"I am influenced in favoring this proposition, first, Restoration
because, I think it is but just that the home of the Jewish Inspiration
people should be restored to them, and, second, for senti- to Nations.
mental reasons.   Again I think it would also prove an
inspiration to all other people.

"I believe the United States Government ought to For Action
take action on Zionism similar to that of England.   I by Execu-
shall be pleased to see a resolution for a Jewish Home- tive and
land in Palestine introduced and adopted." Congress.

(Signed)   "T. H. CARAWAY."

By Representative Henderson M. Jacoway,
Of Arkansas.

"I am in sympathy with the Declarations of England, Favors Dec-
France, and Italy on the Zionist question.   I believe that larations.
Palestine and the Holy Places of both the Christian and
Jewish religions should be forever removed from Turkish
control.   Jerusalem is the city of the Jews, and why
should they not be the guardians of the City?"

(Signed)   "H. M. JACOWAY."

By Representative William A. Oldfield,
Of Arkansas.

For Zionism with All Americans. "I am glad of the opportunity offered to me by the Zionists of America to express my full sympathy for their cause and, in particular, for the British declaration in favor of a Jewish homeland in Palestine. I am ready to give my support and aid for this worthy movement in behalf of the oppressed Jewish nation. Surely no one would doubt that the Jews deserve their re-establishment on their ancient grounds in accordance with the biblical prophecies and in agreement with the hopes and desires of Israel for two thousand years. This sympathy for Zionism is, in my opinion, prevalent among all Americans who have always been anxious to aid the Jews in their great problems.

Zionism Aim of All Belligerents. "As it appears now, the realization of the Zionist program has become one of the aims of our allies, and it bids fair to become one of the questions at the peace conference after this war. I do not at all doubt that the Allies will do all in their power to help the Jews regain their ancient glory and existence. And who knows but that even our opponents, the enemies of civilization, may finally agree to this condition?

Would See Government Action. "I should be glad to see, at the proper time, the United States taking the same position as was taken by our other Allies on this question. Whether this should be done by a declaration on the part of the Government or through an appropriate resolution by Congress is a matter which may be decided at the time when the proposition will appear in a more concrete form."

(Signed)   "WILLIAM A. OLDFIELD."

By Representative John N. Tillman,
Of Arkansas.

"I am in hearty sympathy with the declarations of our Allies, France, England, and Italy, which favor the removal of Palestine and the City of Jerusalem from the control of the Turkish Government. I should favor action on the part of this Government, in support of this position.

Favors Action by Government.

"I was delighted to hear that the sacred city of the Jews was delivered over into English hands last winter. It will be a happy day when the end of Turkish rule in Jerusalem shall be made permanent. The claim of the Jews to the homeland in Palestine in accordance with the declaration above mentioned, should be honored and established by the great Governments now banded together in a holy crusade against the Germans and the Turks."

Should Honor Jewish Claim.

(Signed)   "JOHN N. TILLMAN."

By Representative Denver S. Church,
Of California.

"I would like to see Palestine become the homeland for the Jews, a little republic operated and controlled by them, and guarded and guaranteed against harm by the great powers of the earth. Palestine should be in the hands of the Jews, for they love it more than any other nation can, and consequently would protect it better, and make the sojourner feel more at home."

Entrust Palestine to Jews.

(Signed)   "DENVER S. CHURCH."

By Representative Charles F. Curry,
Of California.

"Those who believe in the Bible, in the old and in the new testaments, know that the principles of Zionism are based on prophecy and that, in the time of the Lord, the Jews will be re-established in Palestine. As an individual, I hope that time may soon come, although I do not believe there is room in Palestine for all of the Jews of the earth and I do not believe that ten per cent of the Jews of the United States would go there if there were room."

Restoration Bound to Come.

(Signed)   "C. F. CURRY."

6   79

By Representative Eneris A. Hayes,
Of California.

Zionism Natural and Desirable.

"It is both natural and proper that the Jewish nation should desire a country or state predominantly their own. Palestine and Jerusalem are, by tradition at least, the country of the Jewish nation, and I believe that the efforts of the Jewish people to re-establish their home there is not only natural but in all ways desirable."

(Signed) "E. A. HAYES."

By Representative William Kettner,
Of California.

Assertion—for Self-Opportunity Will Benefit Jews.

"I am very strongly in favor of the Zionist movement, and when the opportunity arises I will show my feelings by actions, which I believe will be more effective than words." (Signed) "WILLIAM KETTNER."

By Representative Clarence F. Lea,
Of California.

Favors Zionism—Will Act.

"I approve of the Declaration of sympathy with the Zionist aspirations, as voiced by Hon. Arthur J. Balfour. The racial fidelity, the virility, strength and persistent courage of the Jewish people commands the admiration of every right-thinking man. The contributions of individual Jews of the various nations of the earth give promise of a useful career of Jewish character, when given self-assertion through a Jewish nation."

(Signed) "CLARENCE F. LEA."

By Representative Henry Z. Osborne,
Of California.

"I have no hesitancy in stating that in a general way **Approves** I approve the declaration made by Mr. Balfour of estab- **Declaration.** lishing in Palestine a National Home for the Jewish people.

"I think the establishment of such a home is almost **Idea One** purely sentimental, however, as I doubt if any consid- **of Sentiment.** erable number of Jews in the United States, and per- haps in other countries, would care to avail themselves of such a home." (Signed) "HENRY Z. OSBORNE."

By Representative Richard P. Freeman,
Of Connecticut.

"Among the important questions to be settled in the **Success** treaty of peace, will be the disposition and government **Depends** of Palestine. That country should no longer be under **on Jews.** the Government of Turkey. Whether or not a Jewish nation can be created or re-established in Palestine de- pends upon the Jews who are willing to make it their home and their country.

"I approve of the declarations of England, France **Would** and Italy, and would favor the adoption of a similar **Support** resolution by the Congress of the United States." **Congress Resolution.**

(Signed) "R. P. FREEMAN."

By Representative **John E. Raker**,
Of California.

Supporter. "I heartily approve in every way of the official declaration for a Jewish Home Land in Palestine, as issued by the British, French and Italian Governments. I see every reason for such approval, and cannot, at the present moment, see any possible objection to this step.

Ideal and Practical. "This Declaration should be supported and encouraged because the desire for the return of the persecuted Jews to the land of their ancestors has become almost interwoven with their religion. The Jewish people have been hoping for this solution of the world problem for hundreds of years. It will revive the old Hebrew language as spoken in the days of old. Furthermore, it is a most practical venture. This country, under the rule of the Turk, had not been used to its highest extent agriculturally and otherwise. Within the last thirty-five years, as I understand it, the Jews have brought prosperity into part of that country. The establishment of a Jewish home, therefore, would increase the material value of the land manyfold, if not indeed, effect its spiritual uplift in many ways.

For Government Action Like That of Allies. "I personally can see no objection for the United States Government to take action similar to that taken by the other Governments on this matter, at such time when it would be considered advisable by the proper authorities.

Pledges Support. "I wish to assure you that when an appropriate resolution will be introduced in Congress embodying the sentiments thus expressed I shall give it due consideration, with the view of helping to solve the Jewish problem to the benefit of the Jews.

Favors Zionist Movement. "I consider the Zionist movement for a National Home for the Jews in Palestine a very worthy one. I feel certain that the Jews will do everything in their power to help our Government in this world struggle for Democracy at the same time that they will lend a helping hand to their brethren in helping to build their ancient home."

(Signed) "JOHN E. RAKER."

82

By Representative James P. Glynn,
Of Connecticut.

Offers
Support.

"I want to say that I deeply sympathize with the dreams of the Jewish people for a Jewish homeland in Palestine in accordance with the official Declarations of England, France, and Italy. It will certainly give me pleasure to support such a movement in any way I can."

(Signed) "JAMES P. GLYNN."

By Representative Augustine Lonergan,
Of Connecticut.

Advantages
of National
Self-Ex-
pression.

"I am in agreement with the principles of the statements made on the subject of a Jewish Homeland in Palestine by our associates in the war because I am in favor of any and all peoples seeking to express their desires in a government by themselves, for themselves.

Would
Support
Resolution.
Problem
Jewish One.

"While definite action by the United States Government in the premises is hardly necessary, I think a statement by the Government would be in good taste. Insofar as a resolution by Congress would express the sentiments of Congress, I would favor it, but think as I have indicated, that the whole solution is one to be worked out by the Jewish people."

(Signed) "AUGUSTINE LONERGAN."

By Representative Schuyler Merritt,
Of Connecticut.

Favors
Spirit of
Declaration.

"I do approve of having Palestine a headquarters for Jews, and, so far as practicable, under their rule, assuming in the spirit of the British declaration that nothing should be done to the prejudice of the religious rights of any other people. I therefore do favor the spirit of the British declaration.

Jews En-
titled to
Considera-
tion.

"I should be in favor of any reasonable action by our own Government to safeguard the rights of the Jews, particularly in Palestine, and in any other part of the world, not only because I believe in liberty in general, but because I believe the Jews are a valuable element in the industry and civilization of the world."

(Signed) "S. MERRITT."

By Representative John Q. Tilson,
Of Connecticut.

Will gladly
Support
Movement.

"I am in thorough accord with the official declaration of Secretary Balfour, as endorsed by the Governments of France and Italy, on the subject of the establishment in Palestine of a National home for the Jewish people, and I shall gladly support a movement in that direction.

Jews Will
Safeguard
Palestine.

"Surely the control of the wonderful little country containing within its borders the Holy Places of both Jews and Christians should be permanently kept from the Turk. To whose care could it be more appropriately entrusted than to the descendants of those who made such wondrous history there? Jewish history subsequent to the dispersion from Palestine makes it all the more certain that if restored to those whose forebears made its earlier history glorious, it will be faithfully kept and sacredly guarded for the benefit of all mankind."

(Signed)   "JOHN Q. TILSON."

By Representative Benjamin C. Hilliard,
Of Colorado.

Restoration
Recompenses
for War
Losses.

"I have always had an interest in Zionism and have followed the growth of the movement with a great deal of pleasure. Now that the British Army has driven the Turk from the Holy Land the culmination of this dream of the ages seems probable. The blood shed by the English and French knights upon the spears of Saladin's wild horsemen and the blood shed by the brave English Tommies of General Allenby was not in vain if a new nation be established on the hallowed shores of Palestine.

Anxious
to Help.

"I trust the Zionists will not fail to call on me for any possible service I can render."

(Signed)   "B. C. HILLIARD."

By Representative Edward Keating,
Of Colorado.

"The Zionist movement generally, and the British Declaration particularly, are very desirable, in my opinion, from at least two points of view. *Believes in Rights of Small Nationalities.*

"To start with, it gives practical expression to the realization of the rights of small nationalities, among whom Jews stand out very prominently. Secondly, the formation of a Jewish state in Palestine is desirable because of its geographic location, both economically and internationally. The stronger this state the more advantageous it would be not only to the Jews, but also to the great part of the rest of humanity.

"Personally, I do not have the least doubt that this Jewish Government and nation, once again re-established in the land of its ancestors, would in a short while grow materially and spiritually. My sympathies have always been with the oppressed and downtrodden. I know also that these are the sympathies of the Jews all over. I cannot for a moment imagine how anyone can be opposed to the British Declaration as officially announced by the Honorable Arthur J. Balfour. It is high time that the Jews obtained that which they have long been missing and for which they have been hoping and yearning for centuries and ages. *No Excuse for Opposition.*

"From what I have said we can easily understand that I would be glad to support a resolution for a Jewish homeland in Palestine, provided, of course, it has the sanction of the proper authorities in this country. This precaution and reservation I am compelled to make under present conditions because in matters of such tremendous international import I am willing to be guided and advised by the president of the United States. *Would Support a Resolution with Executive Sanction.*

"Please tell the Zionists of America and of the world that I am very glad to have had this opportunity of expressing my sentiments and opinions to the world on this matter which is so important to all the Jews and not the less desirable to all Americans." *Desirable to All Americans.*

(Signed) "Edward Keating."

By Representative Edward T. Taylor,
Of Colorado.

Favors
Action by
Democratic
Govern-
ments.

"I see no reason why I should not support and vote for any measure of this kind if it ever comes before the House for consideration, and I think I am safe in advising you that I will do so, at least I feel very kindly towards this movement of your race.

"1. I approve the British declaration favoring the re-establishment of the Jewish Homeland in Palestine.

"2. I favor appropriate action by the democratic governments to effect the practical consummation of the above declaration." (Signed) "EDWARD T. TAYLOR."

By Representative Charles B. Timberlake,
Of Colorado.

America
Should Have
Been First
to Act.

"The United States, the birthplace of Democracy, should have been the first rather than the last to have favored by act of its Congress, the re-establishment of the Jewish Nation in their historic land, and I shall welcome the opportunity to support this action already too long delayed." (Signed) "CHAS. B. TIMBERLAKE."

By Representative Albert F. Polk,
Of Delaware.

Congres-
sional Sup-
port to
Movement.

"I am in full sympathy with and approve the official declarations of England, France and Italy on the Zionist question. I favor this declaration because I feel that Palestine and the Holy Places of both the Christian and Jewish religions should never again be under Turkish control. I should be glad to see the United States Government take action in line with the British declaration, but action upon this question must be looked for first from the Executive. Personally, however, I would favor the adoption of an appropriate resolution by Congress favoring the establishment of a Jewish National Center in Palestine. I feel that the efforts of the Jewish people to establish a National Home in Palestine are but natural, and the success of this effort and movement would bring about the realization of that which has been nearest to the Jewish heart since the days their forefathers were driven from Palestine." (Signed) "ALBERT F. POLK."

By Representative Frank Clark,
Of Florida.

"I am thoroughly in favor of establishing a Jewish Homeland in Palestine in accordance with the official declaration of the United States, Great Britain, France and Italy, and will do what I can to accomplish this desire."

Favors Declaration and Offers Aid.

(Signed)   "FRANK CLARK."

By Representative Walter Kehoe,
Of Florida.

"I approve of the Declarations of England, France and Italy, and the expression of our own great President on the Zionist question.

Approves Declaration.

"The Jewish population of this country both in times of Peace and in times of War, have been good and loyal citizens and I fully appreciate their worth."

(Signed)   "WALTER KEHOE."

By Representative Charles R. Crisp,
Of Georgia.

"I am heartily in accord with the proposition to restore Palestine to the Jewish race, as a homeland."

Restore Palestine to Jews.

(Signed)   "C. R. CRISP."

By Representative William W. Larsen,
Of Georgia.

"While I have not given this question any study, yet I see no reason why the Jews should not be given a home in Palestine."

Sees no Reason for Opposition.

(Signed)   "W. W. LARSEN."

By Representative Frank Park,
Of Georgia.

"I have not had time to thoroughly read the booklet regarding the establishment of a Jewish homeland in Palestine, but no doubt America will agree with the declarations of England, France and Italy. The four countries mentioned being allied on issues of great moment, doubtless will stand together on other policies where the majority agree."

United States likely to Follow Allied Action.

(Signed)   "FRANK PARK."

87

By Delegate J. Kunio Kalanianaole,
Of Hawaii.

Restoration Merits Approval.

"I am heartily in favor of the plan of the Allied governments in making Palestine the homeland of the Jewish people. This is an action that all right thinking people will approve.

Belated Recognition of Jewish Birthright.

"I know of nothing that would bring more real joy to the Jewish people, long suffering and persistent, than this belated recognition of their birthright.

Restoration Evidences Good Faith of Allies.

"In addition to this feature, the establishment of the homeland would be a lasting monument evidencing the good faith of the Allied Nations in the greatest war of all times, waged in the interest of humanity and world-wide democracy." (Signed) "J. K. KALANIANAOLE."

By Representative Burton L. French,
Of Idaho.

Restoration Merited by Jews.

"The contribution that the Hebrew race has made to world civilization merits the generous course outlined by Mr. Balfour in the matter of the birthplace of the Jewish people." (Signed) "BURTON L. FRENCH."

By Representative Addison T. Smith,
Of Idaho.

God's Promise no "Scrap of Paper."

"Concerning 'The Establishment of a Jewish Home-land in Palestine,' permit me to say I regard it the most momentous event that has occurred since the beginning of the war. While the political effect is of the greatest significance to the world, this event, so unexpected, is attended with a religious significance of far-reaching results. The student of history must be blind who cannot recognize Divine interposition in the returning of God's ancient people to the 'promised land.' The Ruler of the universe is demonstrating to the world that His word is something more than a 'Scrap of paper.' "

(Signed) "ADDISON T. SMITH."

By Representative Edward E. Denison,
Of Illinois.

"My first desire is that Palestine may be forever taken from the dominion of the Turks. After that, I would be glad to see a Jewish Homeland restored in Palestine under any plan that could be agreed upon by the allied Governments." (Signed) "E. E. DENISON." *Would Approve of Restoration.*

By Representative Charles E. Fuller,
Of Illinois.

"I am pleased to assure you that I fully approve the official declarations of England, France and Italy on the Zionist question as quoted by you. I would also favor action along the same lines by our own Government, and a declaration by the Congress of the United States in favor of the establishment in Palestine of a Jewish National Government, if the Jewish people so desire. *Favors Legislative and Executive Action.*

"In any event, Palestine should never be permitted to revert to the Turks. It is the natural home of the Jewish people and there they should be permitted, if they so desire, to establish a government and a National Home." (Signed) "CHAS. E. FULLER." *Natural Home of Jews.*

By Representative Thomas Gallagher,
Of Illinois.

"I believe that the greatest object of the United States in this war, is, and should be, the bringing of freedom to the various subject races of Europe and Western Asia. *In Line with America's Object in War.*

"I believe that every civilized race and people in the world is entitled to some place in the world which they can call their own, and where they can erect and maintain a state which shall represent their own particular ideas in government, religion, and other matters. I certainly feel that the oldest of oppressed races, a race which has kept its racial consciousness under such adverse conditions and during nearly two thousand years of exile, is entitled at last to be permitted to erect a new Jewish State in the old home of their fathers." *Jews Entitled to State.*

(Signed) "THOMAS GALLAGHER."

89

By Representative William J. Graham,
Of Illinois.

World War
to Safe-
guard Small
Nationalities.

"If the Jewish people desire to return to Palestine and there, in the seat of their former national greatness, re-establish their former home, I am in favor of extending to them the opportunity of doing so. If this world war is not in vain, it will establish the right of every people to preserve its own nationality and to work out its own destiny, unmolested and at peace with its neighbors. If the Jews of the world desire again to establish their nationality in the land made sacred to them by the teachings of their prophets and the dust of their ancestors and by the struggles of their race, then I, for one, am for that movement. Let us, by all means, have equal opportunity for national growth and freedom."

(Signed)   "W. J. GRAHAM."

By Representative Clifford Ireland,
Of Illinois.

Wants
United
States
to Assist.

"I am in hearty accord with the Declarations of England, France, and Italy on the Zionist question. I am in favor of these declarations because it seems to me that Palestine and the Holy Places of the Christian and Jewish religions should be forever removed from Turkish control, and if it be the desire of the Jewish race I am heartily in favor of lending our national influence toward the establishment of a government in Palestine, that is, an independent State, sustained and controlled by men and women of that nationality.

World
Owes
Support.

"The Jewish people have had a career so unusual and wonderful in every way that they richly deserve the assistance of the whole world in carrying forward such an experiment.

Will Help
Jewish
Nation.

"I am very glad of the opportunity to make my sentiments known and will do my utmost to help the Jewish race, or nation, in this movement."

(Signed)   "CLIFFORD IRELAND."

By Representative Niels Juul,
Of Illinois.

"I cannot conceive of a thought more beautiful than the restoration of Palestine, the re-organization and re-construction of the Jewish nation.

Project Attractive.

"When Lord Byron, a hundred years ago, wrote in his famous Hebrew Melodies:—

" 'Oh! weep for those that wept by Babel's stream,
Whose shrines are desolate, whose land a dream.
Weep for the harp of Judah's broken shell;
Mourn—where their God hath dwelt the godless dwell!

" 'And where shall Israel lave her bleeding feet?
And when shall Zion's songs again seem sweet?
And Judah's melody once more rejoice
The hearts that leapt before its heavenly voice?"

"he was no doubt already then mourning the fact that there was no home for the Jewish nation.

"The action of the British Army in Palestine in the last few days in cleaning out, at least in part, the Turks from the promised land should make what has for centuries seemed like a dream, a possibility soon to be realized, and I think that the opportunity to establish the Jewish nation in their old Jewish homeland is so near now as to be almost within reach.

Jewish Re-establishment within Reach.

"I, of course, realize that the return to Palestine by all the Jews is impossible and impracticable, but I am sure that hundreds of thousands of the Hebrew race will avail themselves of the opportunity to live and die in the ancient home of their fathers, possessing as they do a history, a religion and a language which centuries of persecution have been unable to blot out.

Many Jews Will Return.

"It would seem that the questions in Lord Byron's sad songs are about to be answered. Zion's songs shall again seem sweet when 'the tribes of the wandering feet and the weary breast' shall again take possession of the land that once was theirs and let us hope that, under a Jewish flag, it will flow with milk and honey.

Jews to Find Peace.

Jewish
Situation
like
Belgian.

"I favor Zionism because I look upon the Jewish situation as I look upon the Belgian situation. The Jews were dispossessed of their home by force and yet in spite of that force they have managed to preserve through the centuries a language, a literature, and a religion. Therefore, the Government and the Congress of the United States should take action similar to that of England."

(Signed) "NIELS JUUL."

By Representative Medill McCormick, Of Illinois.

Favors Au-
tonomous
Jewish
State.

"It goes without saying that I subscribe to Mr. Balfour's declaration for a homeland for the Jews. But I prefer to go further and to say that we ought to support the creation in Palestine of an autonomous state, to be settled by Jews, to whom its destinies should be confided with clear provision for the rights of others, whether living in the Holy Land or going into pilgrimages to the holy places.

Would
Serve as
Deterrent to
Persecutions
elsewhere.
Does not
Conflict
with
Americanism.

"There is no statement for Zionism and the establishment of a Jewish State so able and so clear as that of my friend, Mr. Justice Brandeis. It should be widely distributed. Doubtless few American Jews would settle in Palestine, but even so, that in no sense answers Justice Brandeis' argument. A Jewish state would afford present security and a sure future for the Jews of eastern Europe and their children, who would settle there; it would serve as a deterrent to the oppression of Jews everywhere; it would open to the world, and guard for generations to come, places of incomparable religious and historic interest to mankind. Since this in no sense militates against the citizenship and Americanism of the Jews in America, I am happy to join my views to that of the others who speak for the Jewish state through your volume."

(Signed) "MEDILL McCORMICK."

By Representative William B. McKinley,
Of Illinois.

"I fully approve of the Declarations of England, France, and Italy, on the Zionist question as officially published by these respective governments. I do so for the one great reason among many others, that I consider these declarations an expression of justice, to the Jews, and perhaps to all other small nationalities.

Declaration an Expression of Justice.

"I certainly favor action by the United States Government in line with the British declaration, now or at any future time, when it may be considered to the best interests of the cause.

For Government Action.

"Should a resolution be introduced into Congress expressing in concrete terms the principles of Zionism and a Jewish Homeland in Palestine, I should be glad to give it its proper consideration, which would naturally depend very largely upon the conditions and circumstances that may exist at that particular time. It is very difficult to forecast such possibilities at the present moment when the course of history is so greatly accelerated.

Proper Consideration for Resolution.

"In general, I consider the efforts of the Jewish people to establish a national home in Palestine, as a very fine sentiment which should receive the support of all well-meaning people no matter what their nationality, religion, or race." (Signed) "W. B. McKinley."

Movement Should Receive Support.

By Representative Martin B. Madden,
Of Illinois.

Would Free
Judaism and
Christianity
from Un-
friendly
Control.

"I am heartily in favor of removing Christian and Jewish religions from Turkish control, and to that end I am in accord with the declaration of Honorable Arthur J. Balfour, Secretary of State for Foreign Affairs of the British Government, sympathizing with the Zionists' aspirations for the establishment of a national home for the Jewish people and pledging the best endeavors of the British Government to facilitate the achievement of that object without in any wise interfering with the civil and religious rights of non-Jewish communities in Palestine, or the rights and political status enjoyed by Jews in any other country.

For
Action by
Govern-
ment.

"The career of the Jewish people is deserving of the assistance of the civilized nations of the world in the accomplishment of their object and I favor a declaration by the Government of the United States similar to that expressed by the other allied nations in favor of the establishment in Palestine of a Jewish national center which will afford recognition to the Jews as a distinct nationality.

Guarantee
Jews from
Persecutions.

"The war in which the world is engaged should result in the liberation of all races and make for government by the people to an extent never known before. The Jews have taken a conspicuous place on the battle fields in the present war; they have been unfaltering in their devotion to the cause of freedom and are entitled to every consideration which will guarantee them immunity in the future from the persecution which has been practised against them in the past."

(Signed)   "MARTIN B. MADDEN."

By Representative William E. Mason,
Of Illinois.

"I am decidedly in favor of the resolution by the Congress of the United States favoring the establishment of a national home for the Jewish people in Palestine. This action was already taken by our co-workers in this war, England, France, and Italy. There should be no delay in making this announcement. The project is entirely in the interest of civil liberty and the proposition made by our co-workers and asked for by the Jews of the world does not contemplate anything that can be construed in any way as depriving those of different religious faiths from exercising their full liberty both as to religion and politics. This is bound to come and I hope I may be able to contribute in a way to bring about this great day.

Favorable Pronouncement Should Be Made without Delay.

"My observation of the past and in the present great crisis where the Jews are helping so loyally in treasure and blood is that every American feels more than ever like doing justice to that people. While in the Senate of the United States I opposed all treaties with Russia until we could have an absolute guarantee from the Czar that American citizens should have protection under American passports, regardless of whether they were Jews or Gentiles. The despotism of the autocrats of Russia have brought that country to its present unhappy situation.

Justice to Jews.

"The United States of America will grow in power and prosperity just in proportion as it stands for human liberty."

(Signed)   "WILLIAM E. MASON."

By Representative Henry T. Rainey,
Of Illinois.

"I sincerely hope that the end of the war will find Palestine under the control and protection of the civilized nations of the world, and unless this happens the victory which we must have will not be complete. I am very much pleased with the idea of establishing a Jewish homeland in this most historic section of the world."

Friend of Movement.

(Signed)   "HENRY T. RAINEY."

By Representative John W. Rainey,
Of Illinois.

Would
Like
Action.

"I approve the British Declaration favoring the re-establishment of the Jewish homeland in Palestine and would like to see action by the democratic Governments to that effect."

(Signed)   "JOHN W. RAINEY."

By Representative William A. Rodenberg,
Of Illinois.

Approves
Declaration.

"The British declaration for a Jewish homeland in Palestine, as seconded and indorsed by the French and Italian Governments, is, in my opinion, a very commendable act which has my entire support and sympathy. The history of the Jewish people shows that the realization of the Zionistic principle is very desirable from many viewpoints. It fits into the eternal arrangement of things. It is advisable and laudable that the Jews be granted their long hoped for dream.

"In agreement with President Wilson and his principles of justice in aiding small nationalities in every way, I should be glad to include the Jewish people among those who are to be aided. This would cause their re-establishment in the Holy land. It has been my policy all along to build up things and try to help new ventures that are worthy, instead of tearing down constantly. In thus giving my help along the lines of the British declaration, I shall again follow these same principles.

Pledges
Support.

"I am in favor of an appropriate resolution to be introduced into Congress embodying the thoughts I have set forth in this statement for the Zionist organization in the United States. Should such resolution, or one similar to it, ever be introduced in Congress, I shall favor it and would vote accordingly."

(Signed)   "WILLIAM A. RODENBERG."

By Representative Adolph J. Sabath,
Of Illinois.

"Breathes there a Jew with soul so dead that it no longer reverberates with the sound of hope for a reconstructed 'Homeland' whence once again Israel may send forth his ideals, his literature and his philosophy for the further enlightenment of the world?

"The time now is pregnant with great possibilities; the resulting birth is what we are concerned with as a practical proposition. **Mere Resolutions Useless.**

"We must not, however, permit our judgment to be warped by sentiment. We must do naught that might in the least prejudice the cause. Though I favor the adoption of resolutions for an autonomous Jewish Government, and though I pledge myself to do all in my power to assist in bringing about a favorable action by the Committee on Foreign Affairs, of which I have the honor to be a member, I realize, nevertheless, that mere resolutions will bring no practical results.

"Wilson, the greatest President of all times, has declared in favor of the sacredness of the right of small nations. In President Wilson we shall undoubtedly find a great factor leading for the cause of freedom, liberty and independence of nations. I would, therefore, prefer to wait for a definite expression on his part. I feel that President Wilson will use every effort in behalf of a cause held sacred and inviolate by him. **Faith in Wilson.**

"All arguments to the contrary notwithstanding, I believe that the re-establishment of Palestine as a home for the Jews will not only fail to prejudice the Jewish position, but in my opinion will help to dignify their station amongst all peoples of the earth, and lend ennobling influence on the countless co-religionists who of necessity must remain in a good many countries, where they live under less advantageous conditions than we of America or England. I believe that in the realization of this venture, the Jewish nation will recover a position that has been denied it throughout centuries of oppression and captivity. Not only from a religious aspect but as an independent nation, the Jews if given the oppor- **Restoration Will Dignify Jewish Position.**

97

tunity will soon relight the flame of their traditional passion for distinctive civilization and enlightened government, and once again those backs bent with oppression will straighten, those talents asleep will awaken to sing, paint, and sculpture, those eyes dimmed with tribulation will clear, and through vision unimpaired will radiate philosophy of brotherhood and government based on compassion, love, equality and progress. Thus will the wondrous race that survived all methods of persecution throughout the weary centuries again emanate warmth of Charity and light of Justice for the guidance of all the world."   (Signed)   "A. J. SABATH."

**By Representative John A. Sterling,
Of Illinois.**

Restore
Palestine
to Jews.

"I am heartily in favor of devoting Palestine to the Jewish people as a homeland. It seems to me that it would be extremely appropriate at this time after that country has been taken from the vandals, to restore it to its original people." (Signed)   "JOHN A. STERLING."

By Representative Loren E. Wheeler,
Of Illinois.

"I am in entire sympathy with the declarations of England, France, and Italy, for a Jewish state in Palestine. I fully approve of this step as an act of justice to those Jews of the world who have no homeland of their own. It was very gratifying to me to read the approval of these declarations given by President Wilson. Unlike some others, I consider the action of the allies in their decision for the re-establishment of the Jewish nation not as a favor or an act of charity to this historic people but rather as an expression of justice and what was duly coming to the Jews. *Act of Justice.*

"In my own estimation, this declaration will serve to the Jews and will be looked upon by them as England looks upon its Magna Charta and as Americans consider the Declaration of Independence. It is probably the greatest event for the Jews of the world since the destruction of the Temple. To be re-established in this old home, to regain this historic land and to rebuild their old state is bound to be the greatest single historical jubilation of the children of Israel. It is so much more so for the reason that they had to wait for it for so many centuries. This long delay of justice to them means so much greater and firmer happiness. *Jewish Magna Charta.*

"This result had to come as soon as President Wilson announced the principle of self-determination of all nations big and small. I felt from the first that this meant the regeneration of the Jewish people. I shall, of course, be very glad to support this principle as applied to the Jewish people both personally and officially." *It Had to Come.*

(Signed) "L. E. WHEELER."

By Representative William E. Cox,
Of Indiana.

Judea
Source of
Christianity.

"For more than thirty centuries unique and alone Judea has stood among the countries of the globe. A nation's greatness is not measured by its gold, its numbers, its mines, mountains, valleys, prairies, armies, bridges, or skyscrapers, but is determined by its ideals, by which it has stood, and the benefits it has conferred on mankind such as Judea has stood for. Rome taught mankind a government of law, Greece gave us the highest, beautiful ideal in life, but it remained for Judea and her people to give mankind the true Christian religion, which is now universally believed in by more than a billion of people inhabiting the earth. These ideals and teachings given to searching mankind makes Judea and her people the greatest on earth.

Jews
Oppressed
for
Centuries.

"Through all the years of the past, from the days of Moses, the great lawyer, down to the present time, the Jews have been as constant to this idea as the stars in their courses, although for the centuries past the iron heel of the oppressor like a juggernaut has mercilessly torn the Jews from their land and scattered them to the four corners of the earth. Yet, wherever he has gone forward he has carried his ideals among all nations and tribes of people.

Affords
Opportuni-
ties to
Express
Ideals.

"But just as Moses has led the Israelites out of bondage, so the Allies are now redeeming Judea from the hand of the unspeakable Turk, as a fitting finale to this World War. Judea should be established as an independent nation, an independent sovereign, with power to govern itself and go forward and complete its ideals of life. I feel that I am expressing the thoughts of the American people, and certainly of those with whom I have discussed this question, that the Government of the United States should use its proper influences in seeing that this Jewish State be created, wherefrom will emanate the teachings and principles of old Judea. I shall always favor that proposition whenever it should be brought in some practical form for my decision.

"To see these ideals brought to a realization is cause sufficient for the Zionist Movement among the Jews of the world, as well as among non-Jews who are acquainted with the situation. However, the formation of a Jewish State, probably a Republic in the Holy Land, must of necessity also be of great material assistance not only to the scattered Jews in various countries, but to all the inhabitants of the world. It is, therefore, no surprise to me that the Zionists received full support from all the Governments of the Allies, including our own country. I am sure that in the course of time Zionism will embrace not only all the members of the Jewish faith and nation, but also all other peoples who will have had an opportunity to learn about its purposes and principles." (Signed) "W. E. Cox." *Understanding of Zionism Insures Support.*

By Representative Henry A. Barnhart,
Of Indiana.

"While I have heard no expression from the Jewish residents of the district I represent I should think they would all be in favor of the re-establishment, in Palestine of a national Jewish center. I can see no reason why such a favor should not be granted to the deserving Jewish people of the world and if such a resolution comes up in the House, I shall vote for it providing, of course, that the Jewish people are favorable to the idea of being classified as a separate people. That is to say, I shall be guided by the wishes of the Jewish people themselves." (Signed) "H. A. BARNHART." *Guided by Wishes of Jews.*

By Representative George K. Denton,
Of Indiana.

"I am heartily in sympathy with the official declarations of England, France, and Italy, on the Zionist question, and I am in favor of action by the United States Government in line with the British declaration, and I think that Congress should adopt a proper resolution in favor of the establishment of such a Jewish national centre. *Favors Government Action.*

"I think the efforts of the Jewish people to establish such a home are very commendable." *Effort Commendable*

(Signed) "GEO. K. DENTON."

101

By Representative Louis W. Fairfield,
Of Indiana.

A Country
for Every
Race.

"I am heartily in favor of the action taken by the British, French, and Italian Governments, favoring a Jewish State in Palestine. To me the Jewish people are in many ways the most wonderful in the world. They are a race without a country, save by adoption. In the eternal fitness of things every race should have a country unless it is willing to lose its identity to that country in which it may happen to be resident.

Would
Support
Resolution
of Sympathy.

"Any expression by the United States Government that would not commit it to a maintenance of a Jewish State by force of arms would meet with my approval. An expression in Congress favorable to the establishment of a national Jewish center which would be the expression of a kindly feeling toward that enterprise would receive my indorsement."

(Signed)   "Louis W. Fairfield."

By Representative Merrill Moores,
Of Indiana.

Palestine
Logical
Home of
Jewish
Nation.

"I have always favored the establishment of a Jewish nation, and have believed that the proper location of such a nation would be in Palestine. I am glad to know that our British, French and Italian allies have made solemn declaration favoring such re-establishment.

Palestine
especially
Fitting for
Jews.

"It is especially fitting that the people whose genius made Palestine the birthplace of the highest religious thought, should occupy the land consecrated by the lives and service of two Jews, Moses, the most eminent of all law-givers and Jesus the Christ, the greatest of all teachers.

To Be
Desired by
All Nations.

"The return of the Holy Land to its ancient people under a constitution guaranteeing full and complete political and religious liberty would promise that what is now desert would become an earthly paradise, would accord with the best sentiment and tradition of Jew and Christian alike and would be a happy outcome of a wicked war, most earnestly to be desired and approved by all nations."   (Signed)   "Merrill Moores."

The American War Congress and Zionism

By Representative Albert H. Vestal,
Of Indiana.

"I am unreservedly and unequivocally in favor of the official Declarations of our Allies for a Jewish Centre in Palestine. I am in entire accord with the principles laid down by the Zionists of the world at Basle and especially with those ideals enunciated at the last convention of the Zionists of America held in Pittsburgh. These principles and ideals are, in my opinion, based to a great degree upon those laid down by the founders of this Republic, and I venture to state that it will be these very principles upon which the Republic of Judea will be founded. It is with this end in view, I believe, that President Wilson has expressed himself as favoring the government. I, therefore, favor this Zionist tendency on the part of the Jews of the world and hope that, in all events, the oppressed members of the Jewish faith will be reinstated in their former homeland which must become a restored land to the valiant Crusaders of the Allied Armies, including the Jewish Legion, who are battling the Turks on this sacred territory. *Pittsburgh Program Accords with American Ideals.*

"With the boys of America fighting as one, soldiers of all races and religions, waging battle against the common foe, it is only an act of justice, an expression of humanity, and a sacred duty on the part of the Christian world to restore a homeland to our oppressed brethren, the Jews. This duty, I deem, is especially in line with the democratic and liberal ideals of the United States. *Act of Justice.*

"Because of the fact that the descendants of the old Jewish nation are today the only people without a country and yet the only people with every country, it appears evident that recognition of their loyalty, their bravery, their sense of justice, and their grim determination to administer justice, be accorded them if we are to be consistent in our appeal to freedom and justice of the world. 'Fighting for Freedom' is the motto of the Allies, and under this flag we will conquer. Let us, therefore, give to the Jews that which is their own. Many of them, particularly in free countries, will undoubtedly prefer to remain where they have migrated to, which will indeed be of benefit to those lands. *Consistent with War-Aims of Freedom and Justice.*

"These sentiments that I have expressed speak in clear terms as to my future actions, if necessary, in behalf of this Zionist movement. Now that President Wilson has followed the lead of the Allies for the Jewish Homeland in Palestine, I think it proper and advisable that the representatives of the American people express themselves to the same effect through an appropriate resolution. I am in favor of this proposition because of the unqualified loyalty and bravery of the Jewish young men who have donned the armor of the Allies and who are making the supreme sacrifice upon the blood-stained fields of France, Belgium, Italy, Turkey, and all of the other fronts."   (Signed)   "ALBERT H. VESTAL."

**By Representative Fred S. Purnell,
Of Indiana.**

"I am in hearty sympathy with the declarations of England, France and Italy on this question.

"We are now engaged in the greatest struggle of all the ages, the avowed purpose of which is to make the world safe for people to live in. We are trying to help those who heretofore have not been able to help themselves. Nothing would seem more fitting than to assist the Jewish people in the accomplishment of their desire of the ages, namely to have a flag of their own and to be a people with some semblance of national identity.

"I shall gladly vote and work for a resolution in Congress for the establishment in Palestine of a Jewish National Center."   (Signed)   "FRED S. PURNELL."

**By Representative Everett Sanders,
Of Indiana.**

"I approve the British declaration favoring the re-establishment of the Jewish Homeland in Palestine.

"I favor appropriate action by the democratic governments to effect the practical consummation of the above declaration."   (Signed)   "EVERETT SANDERS."

By Representative William R. Wood,
Of Indiana.

"I sincerely hope that one of the compensations grow- ing out of this world war will be the taking of Palestine forever away from the possession and control of the Turkish Empire. If this is done, the natural thing, and in my opinion, the proper thing in the reconstruction plan, would be to provide some scheme whereby this whole land could be reinhabited by the Jewish people; thus bringing to a happy realization the dream and the establishment of this world old race. Palestine could thus be made an asylum for the oppressed and would no longer be the fertile field of a tyrannical oppressor."

(Signed) "WM. R. WOOD."

By Representative William R. Green,
Of Iowa.

"The recent victories of the British Army and the success of the Allies elsewhere, will undoubtedly deliver Palestine from Turkish rule, and I should be very glad indeed to have a homeland established for the Jewish people in that country, in accordance with the declarations of the Allies.

"I trust that nothing will happen which will prevent the plans of the Zionists from being carried out to a successful conclusion. You have my best wishes."

(Signed) "W. R. GREEN."

By Representative Harry E. Hull,
Of Iowa.

Palestine Best for Jewish State.

"If the Jewish people desire to establish an independent sovereignty in Palestine, the Allied nations should aid them in accomplishing this object. The Jews long since have established their worthiness to have a country they can call home and there could be no more fitting place for them to reunite as a race than in that ancient land from which they sprang.

Let Jews Develop Nationally.

"The Jewish race has occupied a position in the history of the world peculiar to itself. Although its peoples have had no country where sentiment could be unified and national pride developed, they have maintained their characteristics and have proven virile factors in all of the nations to which they have been attached. Give them a sovereignty of their own and they would have the opportunity to develop nationally as they have never had since the ancient days of the race.

Interests not Antagonistic to Our Own.

"I am in sympathy with the Declarations made by the British, French, and Italian governments. I take it from the public utterances of the Honorable Arthur J. Balfour of England, that the object is to create an independent government for the Jews and the mere fact that these Allied countries have sanctioned such a movement insures to the world that no nation would be established whose interests would be inimical to our own.

America Should Endorse and Assist Movement.

"I believe the United States should heartily endorse the movement and lend its active aid to see that this end is attained. I believe that some comprehensive plan should be outlined so that when the final summing up shall come in this great war, Palestine shall be turned over to the Jewish people so that it can become one of the great national democracies of the world."

(Signed)   "HARRY E. HULL."

By Representative Horace M. Towner,
Of Iowa.

"I most heartily and unreservedly approve the Zion- ist movement and endorse the declarations of England, France, and Italy recently made, favoring the propositions.

"Ever since I first heard of the aspirations of the Jew- ish people in this regard, I have given it my heartiest and most sympathetic approval. To rid the Holy Land of the Moslem rule, and to restore the sacred soil to the people who made it sacred should appeal to every man who loves justice and hates oppression and persecution.

"I am in favor, by such means as would be appro- priate, of placing the United States in line with the action already taken by Great Britain, France and Italy. As the action taken by those governments was not the action of their parliaments, I am not sure that a resolution of Congress would be appropriate action. But whatever would be the proper procedure, I will favor it. I think it would be advisable to consult the President and the Secretary of State as to the matter.

"No one who is in sympathy with the cause of the Allies but must have felt a thrill of gratitude and exultation when the news came of the expulsion of the Turks and the triumphant entry of the Allies into Jerusalem. Americans without regard to race will rejoice when the glad hour shall come, as come it surely will, when under a protectorate of the nations, the Jews shall again regain and forever occupy their old home, Palestine, that holds so much of the reverence and love of mankind."

(Signed)   "H. M. Towner."

By Representative Frank P. Woods,
Of Iowa.

For Rehabilitation of Small Peoples.

"I do not see any possible objection that can be made by any American against the British declaration favoring a Jewish State in the Holy land. It seems to me that it would guarantee equal political status to Jews in any other country. I believe that the Jewish people as a result of this war ought to regain their nationality. I thoroughly believe that an independent Jewish State should be established in the land of their ancestors. Aside from the strong sentimental reasons for establishing such a state I believe there are many practical reasons for the project. I have always favored and supported the principles underlying the movement for the rehabilitation of small nationalities and shall feel it my duty to support this cause whenever given an opportunity."

(Signed) "FRANK P. WOODS."

By Representative Daniel R. Anthony, Jr.,
Of Kansas.

For Autonomous Government in Palestine. For European Jews.

"I am in favor of the establishment of an autonomous government in Palestine to be administered by the people of that country.

"As far as a Jewish Homeland is concerned such a project might be feasible for the Jews in Europe, but the Jewish citizens of the United States are so firmly established here and are so desirable as American citizens that I cannot conceive of any extensive colonization of Palestine from America."

(Signed) "D. R. ANTHONY, JR."

By Representative W. A. Ayres,
Of Kansas.

"Like President Wilson, I firmly believe in the rights
of smaller nations, or nationalities rather, because I believe they have a right to make and determine their own
future destiny. A people, regardless of race or religion,
should be able to claim some definite territory as their
domain, or their native land.

"The Jewish people have given to history many eminent men and women, not only during the early period of
the history of the world but since modern civilization has
sprung up, and I feel that the Jewish people of today
will feel that they have a spot—a place they can call their
land, if the plans of the Zionists are carried out.

"I heartily approve the declarations of England,
France and Italy in the matter of the establishment of a
national home for Jewish people in Palestine, for the
reasons that I have just given, and I believe our American
Government should favor the indorsements given to this
move by our sister countries, and should so show its
interest, by the introduction of a resolution in the
National Congress.

"I am sure that a Jewish nation established in historic
old Palestine will result in blessing and benefit to every
Jew of today and by the formation of a national home for
the Jews, a better understanding and co-operation will
come about with all the established nations of the world."

(Signed)   "W. A. Ayres."

By Representative Philip P. Campbell,
Of Kansas.

"I strongly sympathize with the important movement
having for its object the establishment of a Jewish Homeland in Palestine, in accordance with the official declarations of England, France and Italy, and my best wishes
go out for the success of those who are devoting their
efforts toward that end."

(Signed)   "Philip P. Campbell."

By Representative Guy T. Helvering,
Of Kansas.

Unanimous for Jewish National Aspiration.

"In company with all Americans I have rejoiced in the recent triumphs which have given assurance of the redemption of Palestine, and I believe that the practically unanimous sentiment of America and her Allies is that advantage should be taken of the opportunity to forward the national and beneficial aspirations of the Jewish people. With that sentiment I am in hearty accord.

Ungrateful not to Aid Zionism.

"Every student of American history is aware of the great contributions made to the progress of our country by the children of Zion. In war they have given to us freely of their blood and treasure and in peace they have been equally patriotic in every movement destined to advance the best interests of the country. Therefore, we would indeed be ungrateful did we not wish to aid them, now when the time and the opportunity is here to gratify their desire to regain the land of their fathers and there build up a government which will be their own, in the best sense of one which will be a valuable addition to the family of nations. That this result may soon be achieved is my hope and my belief."

(Signed)   "GUY T. HELVERING."

By Representative Edward C. Little,
Of Kansas.

"I approve of the official Declarations of England, *Right of* France and Italy. Why? Because the Jewish people *Nationalism Inherent in* have the same right to a national organization as any *Every* people, indeed, the miraculous way in which they have *People.* maintained themselves for centuries scattered over the earth emphasizes the equity of granting them that nationality. Furthermore, the loyalty of the Jewish-American people to this country has been such that they are entitled to every consideration from our nation.

"I would favor an appropriate resolution by Congress *For* expressing the principles of Zionism. *Congress Resolution.*

"During my visit to Jerusalem, a quarter of a century ago, I rode from Hebron to the Holy Land. As the night *Land Must* fell I stopped at the tomb of Rachael and watched the last *be Restored* rays of the sun decline beyond the hills of Judea, and *to Jews.* ever since there has been fixed in my mind that tomb which for centuries had been held sacred by Jews, Mohammedans, and Christians—the mother of your great race. I would like to see a returned Judea, with a splendid monument erected at that modest sepulchre, to typify the world's respect for her whom Jacob buried by the wayside on the road to Bethlehem."

(Signed)   "E. C. LITTLE."

By Representative James C. Cantrill,
Of Kentucky.

Free
People
Favor Dec-
laration.

"The action of the British Government favoring the establishment in Palestine of a national home for the Jewish people will meet with the approval of all free people in all parts of the world. I have read with much interest and profit the Zionists' publications, and heartily endorse them in every way."

(Signed)   "J. C. CANTRILL."

By Representative Swagar Sherley,
Of Kentucky.

Approves
Restoration.

"I should be very glad to see the Jewish people establish a homeland in Palestine."

(Signed)   "SWAGAR SHERLEY."

By Representative H. Garland Dupré,
Of Louisiana.

Recognizes
Justice of
Claim.

"I may say in a general way that I am in sympathy with the Zionist Movement, and hope that in the adjustment of post-war conditions the historic and just claims of Palestine to recognition will not be overlooked by our own country and our Allies."

(Signed)   "H. GARLAND DUPRÉ."

By Representative Albert Estopinal,
Of Louisiana.

"It seems to me most natural and plausible that the *One of* *War's Aims.* Zionist movement should meet with the earnest approval of the leading statesmen of the world. The recent Declaration of their intention of assisting it physically as well as morally is only in keeping with one of the vast and noble aims of this war, to wit: self-determination and self-government for the oppressed and dispersed of the earth.

"The plan of reuniting the Jewish race under a government all their own in the very land which was once theirs and of which they were despoiled by a barbarous conqueror is a lofty one. It merits our individual sympathy and co-operation. It deserves in every way the confidence and support of the great governments and their peoples who are now waging against Teutonic and Turkish oppressor this war of liberation and justice. *Lofty Movement— Deserves Co-opera-tion.*

"The Jews themselves should be a unit in approving and applauding so momentous a step. It is in fact a tribute paid by civilization to that spirit of homogenity and racial affinity which is theirs and on which is based the effort of moulding into self-governing units the fragments of dismembered nations. *United Jewry Should Approve.*

"However separated by time, distance, and custom the individual Jew may be from his brother, their blood and their ideals have remained unchanged after centuries of suffering and abuse, and their desire (an ancient one) to get together betokens an aim on their part potential with great and happy possibilities. *Jewish Ideals Have Remained Unchanged.*

"I heartily endorse the declarations of Great Britain, France and Italy as recently expressed looking toward the foundation of a free and independent Hebrew nation and will do all that lies in me to make it a reality." *Will Aid in Establish-ment of Nation.*

(Signed)   "ALBERT ESTOPINAL."

By Representative Whitmell P. Martin,
Of Louisiana.

Favors
Declaration.

"I beg to state that the plan of the British Declaration meets with my entire approval.

Duty of
America to
Assist.

"The Jewish people of this country have responded most promptly and notably in the prosecution of this war, and I deem it the duty of this country to facilitate in every way the achievement of the object and purpose of the Zionists in the establishment of a National Home for the Jewish people." (Signed) "W. P. MARTIN."

By Representative John T. Watkins,
Of Louisiana.

For Jewish
Welfare.

"I take great interest and have much friendship for the Jews, and anything which may be conducive to their welfare, happiness and prosperity meets with my most hearty approval and sincere approbation."

(Signed) "J. T. WATKINS."

By Representative Louis B. Goodall,
Of Maine.

National
Home Advantageous.

"I favor the establishment of a Jewish homeland in Palestine. I think it a good plan for the Jewish people to have a country which will be to them a National Home, and which will be their refuge when persecuted by other nations.

Favors
Action by
Executive
and Congress.

"I should be glad to see action by our Government, and a resolution in Congress, favoring these principles.

Interests
all Jews.

"I think the Jews all over the world should be intensely interested in establishing a National Home."

(Signed) "LOUIS B. GOODALL."

By Representative Wallace H. White, Jr.,
Of Maine.

"The desire of the Jewish people to re-establish the Jewish nation in Palestine, the land of their origin, and the endorsement of the movement to this end voiced by England, France, Italy and by many leaders of thought in this country meet with my approval. What may be called racial instinct inheres in every people but it has never seen more persistent expression than by the Jews. Through many centuries representatives of the race have made a powerful impression upon the business, the social and the political thought and life of every other nation. It is surely an anomaly that such a race should be without nationality.

"It seems to me that the plan proposed should receive at some appropriate time the approval of this Government. I hope that through the kindly offices of the nations of the world supplementing the efforts of Jewish people themselves, Palestine may be restored to them and a Jewish nation with national ideals, hopes and aspirations may be founded."

(Signed) "WALLACE H. WHITE, JR."

By Representative Charles P. Coady,
Of Maryland.

"I approve the Declarations of England, France and Italy on the Zion question, and my reasons are similar to those expressed by the governments mentioned.

"I would like to see action on this question either by the Executive or by Congress.

"I view with favor the efforts of the Jewish people to establish a national home in Palestine. This matter should, however, be determined by the Jewish people themselves, and their desires in this respect should govern."

(Signed) "CHARLES P. COADY."

Margin notes (White): Until Restoration Jewish Position Anomalous. — Hopes to See Government Action.

Margin notes (Coady): Approves Declarations. — Favors Government Action. — For Self-Determination.

By Representative Jesse D. Price,
Of Maryland.

Justice at last for Jews.

"The declarations for a Jewish Homeland in Palestine by the British, French and Italian Governments as well as the sympathetic letter of President Wilson on the Zionist movement comprise some of the most important developments in the history of this war. It is undoubtedly the greatest event in the diaspora of the Jews in the last two thousand years. It indicates once for all that world consciousness has finally taken a fair attitude regarding the Jewish problem. It is with the greatest gratification that I have learned of these events in the last year.

Zionism Solution of Jewish Problem.

"There have been many ways proposed to solve the much perplexed Jewish question. However, very few leaders in Europe, outside perhaps of the Jews themselves, struck upon the idea that the only original and real end to this problem, and its most satisfactory solution, rests not in charity or even freedom and equality among nations but in the re-establishment of the old Kingdom of Judea where the Jews may be allowed to solve their own problems and take an interest in the welfare of the Jews elsewhere. It is thus another glad sign of the times that we have come to realize the true significance of this Zionist movement. It is now practically universally accepted not only among the Jews of the world but among Christians and even Mohammedans.

"I am glad that the President of the United States, the great Executive of this free republic, has seen fit to express his great interest in this Jewish movement, thus also speaking in the name of the American people.

Friend; Willing to Help in Congress.

"As far as I am concerned, I shall be glad to aid the realization of the solution to this problem in whatever method that I may be in position to participate in. Judging from past experiences, I am sure that the American Congress, should it become necessary and advisable, will speak its thoughts for Zionism, even as it did during the time of the abrogation of the Russian Treaty. This may, perhaps, not be necessary for it is possible that the question will be settled by the conferees at the peace table in favor of the Jews without any further trouble."

(Signed)   "JESSE D. PRICE."

By Representative Frederick N. Zihlman,
Of Maryland.

"I beg to say that the Jewish people have such a wonderful record as a race, and they certainly deserve the assistance of the Great Powers to show their powers of self-government.

Powers Should Help Secure Self-Government to Jews.

"If the Jewish people themselves desire to establish a government in Palestine, such as has been suggested I am in favor of lending our national influence toward such a movement.

"Trusting this is satisfactory, I beg to remain,

(Signed)   "F. N. ZIHLMAN."

By Representative Frederick W. Dallinger,
Of Massachusetts.

"I am heartily in favor of the declaration of our Allies upon the Zionist question.

Favors Declaration.

"I believe that Palestine which is so dear to religious people all over the world, should be forever freed from Turkish rule and should be granted an independent government under the protection of the civilized nations of the earth.

Keep Palestine Free from Turks.

"While action on the part of our government ought to come in the first instance from the Executive, nevertheless, I favor the adoption of a resolution by Congress expressing the views of our national legislators in favor of the establishment of a national center of the Jewish race in the Holy land."

For Congress Resolution.

(Signed)   "FREDERICK W. DALLINGER."

By Representative James A. Gallivan,
Of Massachusetts.

Restoration Will Secure Self-Expression to Jewish Idealists.

"Those who are even slightly acquainted with my work in Congress all these years in behalf of the Jews and other oppressed and small nationalities, will clearly understand my attitude on the question of a Jewish homeland in Palestine as pronounced by the governments of Great Britain, France and Italy. I have been interested in the Zionist movement for many years and have expressed my sentiments in its favor on many occasions even before our Allied Governments issued their declaration. I am, therefore, unqualifiedly in favor of those official declarations, and am ready to go even further and state that I desire to see Palestine re-established as an independent Jewish state where the great Jewish idealists may be in a position to preach their doctrine to the world unmolested. The British declaration is merely a practical consummation of the true and lofty principle underlying the entire Zionist movement.

Zionist Principles Coincide with American.

"I know that the great Jewish leaders of America, the true loyal Americans of Jewish faith, are giving their heart and soul to this noble cause. The Zionists of America may truly be proud to have in their midst such persons as Justice Brandeis, Rabbi Wise, Judge Mack, Professor Frankfurter, Mrs. Fels, and numerous others just as worthy, which space does not permit to enumerate. The principles of Zionism in many ways, it appears to me, coincide with the principles of America and when these democratic principles, as laid down by President Wilson, will be realized, then we pray and hope that the Zionist principles will also become actualities.

For Action by Executive and Legislature.

"I firmly believe that our Government ought to take the same attitude on this Zionist question as was taken by the other Allied Governments. I do not doubt that such will be the action of the United States whenever the proper moment will arrive. The explicit and unqualified indorsement by President Wilson for the small nationalities of the world make this step in the future almost a certainty. I also believe that Congress

118

ought to pass an appropriate resolution expressing its sympathies and support with the Zionist principles and the British declaration for a Jewish centre in the Holy Land, in the land of Israel."

(Signed) "JAMES A. GALLIVAN."

By Representative Alvan T. Fuller,
Of Massachusetts.

"Without knowing much about the details of the Zionist movement I can say unqualifiedly that I am in favor of it. In view of the fact that the Jewish people are so discriminated against and because they, as the Bible declares, are His chosen people, and He chose a Jewish woman to be the Mother of His only son, it is my conviction that the Jewish race is entitled to this consideration. Jews Entitled to Consideration.

"I am proud that at this time when our nation is fighting for the rights of smaller nationalities to say that I am heartily in favor of action on this question by the United States, and will be pleased to vote for an appropriate resolution by Congress to establish a Jewish National Centre in the House. War Fought for Small Nationalities.

"I am glad of the opportunity to express my views on this matter."

(Signed) "ALVAN T. FULLER."

By Representative Frederick H. Gillett,
Of Massachusetts.

"It seems to me most fitting that Palestine, to which nearly all the people of the civilized world turn with a sentiment of reverence, should again be under the control of her native people, whose dispersion has been the means of bringing home to all the nations among whom they have been scattered their brilliant qualities of organization and thrift and indomitable energy and capacity for achievement. I hope the Zionist program will be successfully carried out, as it will gratify both the sentiment and sound judgment of the world." Realization Will Give Play to Capacity for Achievement.

(Signed) "FREDERICK H. GILLETT."

By Representative William S. Greene,
Of Massachusetts.

Are Entitled to Fullest Opportunities as a Law-Abiding People.

"I approve of the official Declaration of England, France and Italy on the Zionist question.

Reasons for Approval.

"My reasons are that I think the Jewish population throughout the world have shown great courage and loyalty to their faith, and to their people, under the most trying circumstances and hardship. Palestine is their Fatherland and they are entitled to the fullest protection there, in order that they may enjoy the rights both civil and religious that law abiding people throughout the world are entitled to.

For Action by United States.

"I think the United States Government should join hands with the Allied Governments in making the British declaration effective at the earliest moment.

For Congress Resolution.

"I am in favor of the adoption of an appropriate resolution by Congress in favor of the establishment in Palestine of a Jewish National Centre.

Zionism Should be Encouraged.

"I believe the efforts of the Jewish people to establish a National Home in Palestine should be encouraged. I favor it heartily as a measure of justice, and memorial to their breadth of spirit during their long years of trial and persecution." (Signed) "WILLIAM S. GREENE."

By Representative George Holden Tinkham,
Of Massachusetts.

Favors Realization of Movement.

"I approve the British Declaration favoring the reestablishment of the Jewish Homeland in Palestine and would like to see this movement realized."

(Signed) "GEORGE HOLDEN TINKHAM."

By Representative Wilfred W. Lufkin,
Of Massachusetts.

"I am very glad to endorse the movement for the adoption by the United States of the declarations of England, France and Italy in favor of the establishment in Palestine of a National Home for the Jewish people.

For American Indorsement.

"The history of the accomplishments of the Jews during the past two thousand years under the most trying conditions with which any race has ever been obliged to contend, speaks for itself. The conduct and progress of the race in our own Republic in recent years is further evidence of the character of the people and their ability to conserve their best traditions, even under the most adverse circumstances.

History of Jews Speaks for Itself.

"This war is being fought for the purpose of lifting the yoke of oppression and tyranny from every nation and race and of making this old world of ours a better and a happier abode for all mankind. When the time for re-establishment and reorganization arrives, I can think of no more righteous result of this terrible conflict than the restoration to the Jews of their old home, which they once presided over with such grace, refinement, dignity and efficiency. Moreover, such action will likewise bring about the greatly desired result, of making impossible a repetition of Turkish rule with all its horrors over the Palestine of the future.

War Fought to Lift Yoke of Oppression.

"I shall gladly favor in the House of Representatives the passage of a resolution favoring the establishment of such a Jewish National Center in Palestine and I wish you the utmost success in your very worthy movement."

Favors Congress Resolution.

(Signed) "W. W. Lufkin."

By Representative Richard Olney,
Of Massachusetts.

Enthusiastic over Declarations.

"I am very glad to express my approval, in fact my enthusiasm, for the official Declarations by our Allied countries in favor of a Jewish Homeland in Palestine. I was especially delighted to read the letter of President Wilson in which he expresses much interest in the Zionist movement, not only in the United States, but all over the world.

Americanism and Zionism Similar Expressions.

"The purposes of Zionism, the return to Palestine of many of its former original inhabitants, has exceptional possibilities for many Jews in less favored countries. The democratic principles, as outlined by the Zionist leaders of America, may be said in part not only to include the genuine American ideals and desires, but also to supplement these lofty thoughts. Americanism and Zionism, when both are clearly understood and rightly pursued, express a common cause from many viewpoints.

Glad American Jewry is Zionistic.

"I am glad to see that American Jewry has awakened to its task and duties to extend a helping hand for the establishment of a Jewish State for so many of their unfortunate brethren, as well as a spiritual centre for the Jews all over the world. As an American, and as a believer in the principles laid down by America and its Allies, in this world war, I shall be pleased to aid in the realization of the cause of Zionism."

(Signed)   "RICHARD OLNEY."

By Representative Allen T. Treadway,
Of Massachusetts.

"It is with pleasure that I endorse the statement of Senator Henry Cabot Lodge* in which he so heartily approves the declarations of England, France and Italy on the Zionist question. I wish the Jewish people all success in their undertaking to establish a National Home in Palestine."   (Signed)   "ALLEN T. TREADWAY."

Indorses Lodge Statement.

By Representative Calvin D. Paige,
Of Massachusetts.

"The history of the Jews is perhaps richer in high romance than that of any other people and from that point of view, if from no other, the re-establishment of this great race in the cradle land of its origin and of its great contributions to the religion and civilization of the world, would be one of the normal and logical consequences of the winning of the world war by the Allies.

Logical Result of Victory.

"I am very glad to endorse the broad visioned declaration of the Right Honorable Arthur James Balfour, the British Secretary of State for Foreign Affairs, in behalf of his government, and that has been affirmed by the governments of France and Italy, and I hope soon to see our own government make a declaration in accord with that of our great European Allies.

Supports British Statement.

"The persecution of the Jews has been a disgrace to and blot upon the history of civilization. The opportunity and occasion are seemingly both at hand when this virile people shall and can have its historic home restored to its charge and keeping, with all that that implies, out of the rich inspiration of its history and achievements."

Restoration now in Sight.

(Signed)   "CALVIN D. PAIGE."

---

* See statement by Senator Lodge, page 43.

By Representative John J. Rogers,
Of Massachusetts.

Approves
Declaration.
"I cordially approve the official Declarations of the Governments of England, France and Italy, on the question of a Jewish Homeland in the Holy Land.

Jews Logical
Guardians of
Country.
"I am convinced that the time has come when justice must be rendered to the Jew, not in any charitable or haphazard fashion, but on broad and permanent lines. This may best be rendered by the re-establishment of the Jews in Palestine. This land was that of the birth of their nation, their culture, and their religion. They are, therefore, the logical people to guard and control that country where the sacred treasures of Christianity as well as of Judaism are found. The Zionists of the world, in accordance with the British Declaration, should do nothing to prejudice the civil and religious rights of the non-Jewish population in Palestine. (Signed)   "JOHN J. ROGERS."

By Representative William W. Venable,
Of Massachusetts.

Approves
Declara-
tions.
"I am glad to give my approval and consent to the declarations for Zionism and the Jewish homeland in Palestine as officially issued by the British, French and Italian Governments.

Grips
Imagination.
"The idea of the re-establishment of a Jewish government is one that grips the imagination and it is one that appeals to me as a matter of sentiment.

Faith in
United
States
Government.
"As to the advisability of our government issuing a declaration similar in character to those of France, Italy and Great Britain, I am unable to say at this time. I am confident, however, that at the proper time our government will do the proper thing.

Support of
All America.
"As I understand it, the Zionist movement is an effort to accomplish one of the great ideals of a great race. As such it will receive the approval and endorsement as well as support of the people of America."

(Signed)   "W. W. VENABLE."

By Representative Joseph Walsh,
Of Massachusetts.

"It would seem to me to be most fitting that a National Home for the Jewish people be established at
Palestine, not to interfere with the rights of non-Jewish
precincts in that land, nor to prejudice the rights of the
Jewish people residing in other nations. No more appropriate spot could be selected for this long hoped for
result. The Jewish people have played a prominent part
in the world's history, and in the upbuilding of every
land. They have realized what freedom, as guaranteed
by our government means, and in the historic land of
Palestine, so linked with the early history of the Jewish
people, it would, as I have said, seem peculiarly appropriate that they be secured a National home.

Jews Understand Free Government.

(Signed)   "JOSEPH WALSH."

By Representative Samuel W. Beakes,
Of Michigan.

Palestine Belongs to Jews.
"I know that the American people of non-Jewish persuasion were just as pleased as were the American Jewish people, or as were the Jews all over the world when the news reached us that England had captured Palestine from the Turks, and later that England had promised to help the restoration of the Jewish nation on that land. It has been a constant source of regret to all of us that Palestine has remained in the hands of the Turks for so long. We shall now be glad to do anything to restore it to those who have been driven out of the Holy Land and who have suffered through persecution in other lands. This cause for the establishment of a Jewish State in Palestine ought to be pleasing to Americans.

Of Benefit to World but Essential to Jews.
"I should not hesitate to say that the principles underlying Zionism are just and praiseworthy from every angle, and should get the indorsement, if not indeed the support of the Jews and non-Jews alike. I am, therefore, glad to have this pleasant opportunity to give my unqualified support to the official Declarations of England, France and Italy. I hold this movement to be essential to the Jewish people and one that would prove beneficial to the entire civilized world.

Will Support Congress Resolution.
"I would be glad to vote for a proper resolution embodying the thoughts I have just expressed, if brought up in Congress, especially if this resolution will have the sanction of the State Department, as I believe it is bound to have."

(Signed) "Samuel W. Beakes."

By Representative Gilbert A. Currie,
Of Michigan.

"Please convey to the Zionists of America my entire sympathy and indorsement of the Declaration made by the Honorable Arthur J. Balfour, Secretary of State for Foreign Affairs, in the name of the English Government, favoring the establishment in Palestine of a national home for the Jewish people. I see every reason for supporting this Declaration because I am anxious to aid in the just solution of the much vexed Jewish problem. It seems to me that the establishment of the Jewish state in their ancient home will, more than anything else, bring about the proper solution. It is particularly gratifying to note that this Declaration makes the distinct stipulation that 'nothing shall be done which may prejudice the civil and religious rights of non-Jewish communities in Palestine, or the rights and political status enjoyed by Jews in any other country.' *Supports Balfour Declaration.*

"I agree with you that in view of President Wilson's utterances in favor of the rights of all small nationalities which are to be given the opportunity of determining their own futures, it is fair and proper, in fact absolutely necessary, that the Jews be given this right and be accorded these privileges. Accordingly, I should be glad to cast my vote for and support an appropriate resolution that may be introduced in Congress purporting these ends. *"Rights of Small Nationalities" Includes Jewish People.*

"I am fully aware of the fact that only a very small percentage of the American Jews will return to their ancient national home in Palestine, nor is it necessary or desirable that American Jews should return. However, for those who will return from other countries it surely will be a blessing and the realization of a life-long dream, and to those who will remain in those countries where they have already become acclimatized, it will undoubtedly cause much pride and happiness to know that once for all the Jewish flag is to wave in the historic City of Jerusalem."   (Signed)   "GILBERT A. CURRIE." *Source of Pride to All Jews.*

By Representative Frank E. Doremus,
Of Michigan.

A Welcome
Opportunity
to Realize
National
Aspirations.

"I have carefully read the declaration of Honorable Arthur J. Balfour, Secretary of State for Foreign Affairs of the British Government, and am pleased to give it my cordial approval. I am in hearty sympathy with the efforts of the Jewish people to establish a national domicile in Palestine, subject, of course to the limitation that nothing be done which would be prejudicial to the civil and religious rights of non-Jewish people resident therein. While many Jews who have acquired honor, distinction, and fortune in America will desire to continue their residence among us, the consummation of this very worthy project would afford a welcome opportunity to all those who desire to realize this national aspiration."

(Signed) "FRANK E. DOREMUS."

By Representative Joseph W. Fordney,
Of Michigan.

Unhampered
Spiritual
Development
for All
Peoples.

"I approve the declaration of England, France, and Italy, on the Zionist question. Because I wish everybody, all classes of people, to worship God according to the dictates of their conscience.

Congress
Resolution
Would be
Appropriate.

"I favor action by the United States Government in accordance with the principles of Zionism. I believe the adoption of a resolution by Congress in favor of the establishment in Palestine of a Jewish National Centre would be appropriate, especially at this time."

(Signed) "J. W. FORDNEY."

By Representative Edward L. Hamilton,
Of Michigan.

"I am now writing this without adequate detailed information before me as to just how much territory has already been occupied in Palestine under the stimulus of the Zionist Movement and how the problems of Government are purposed to be solved. My recollection is that a considerable fund was created some years ago, raised largely by contributions in small sums by Jews throughout the world, in aid of this movement; that the fund is constantly increasing and that the Movement is achieving substantial results in the purchase, occupation and improvement of lands.

Achievements in Land Improvement.

"The idea of a Jewish Homeland in Palestine has appealed to me ever since I first read of the Zionist Movement. It has its practical aspects as furnishing a possible substantial habitation, especially for those who have been driven from their homes in Central Europe by the War, and it appeals to the imagination in ways that are obvious."

Zionism Appeals.

(Signed)   "E. L. HAMILTON."

By Representative Patrick H. Kelley,
Of Michigan.

Zionism of International Import.

"With the Declaration of Great Britain in favor of Zionism, the first and most important official step for a Jewish Homeland in Palestine was announced to the world. Generally speaking, it brought forward the Jewish National movement as an international problem. Zionism was, up to that time, known and seriously debated only among those who were interested in it because of racial or religious reasons; it hardly stepped out of the gates of the Ghetto. This War has put this movement as one of the aims of the Allied powers, and widened the scope of Jewish Nationalism—it put it on an international basis. Its principles have been officially accepted by the United States, England, France, Italy, and our smaller allies.

Zionism Conquered Public Opinion.

"Zionism has apparently conquered public opinion in all liberal lands, among Jews and Gentiles. It appeals not only to the idealism of the world, but also to its political interests, economic possibilities, and cultural aspirations. The Zionist Declaration has much in store for the free countries of the world, and, naturally, even more to the Jews of the world.

Revival of Hebrew Inspiring.

"I am told that Hebrew, the language of the prophets, is to be the official means of communication in the New Jewish State. This decision appeals very favorably to one's imagination—the revival of a language that had been adjudged dead by many for so many centuries. It is as inspiring even as the rebirth of the ancient land and people of Israel." (Signed) "PATRICK H. KELLEY."

The American War Congress and Zionism

By Representative Harold Knutson,
Of Minnesota.

"For several years I have followed quite closely the movement for the re-establishment of a Jewish state. I first became interested in the Zionist movement as a student of political history, and in the course of time it became one of the subjects which I deemed worthy of study. Under these conditions it is hardly necessary for me to say that I am absolutely and unqualifiedly in favor of the British, French and Italian Declarations for the establishment of a Jewish center in the Holy Land. Personally, I will go further to say that I would like to see created, in the ancient land of Israel, a free, independent and democratic Jewish republic wherein a goodly number of Jews would enjoy the privileges and rights that so many of them were deprived of in their long history of repression and suppression. I feel that this will eventually come about, perhaps at the end of this great war, which cannot but result in a better, freer and a more perfect world.

Unqualified Indorsement by Student of Political History.

"Why do I believe this? It is because I know that the Jews are a very strong and virile people who are bound to accomplish their long-cherished ambition. Their tenacity and resistance through all ages is shown clearly by their ability to remain and persist without being absorbed and assimilated in all these centuries, during which time so many other peoples and nations have become lost and forgotten; I am for this movement because the Jews have been looking forward to the re-establishment of Judea for many centuries; they have been praying for it day after day; they have been yearning for their ancient home in their ancient land; I am with the Zionists, furthermore, because I believe that the formation of a Jewish state is the great, the greatest single settlement of the Jewish question which would have its effects in Palestine and out of it.

Best Solution of Problem for Jews Everywhere.

Extend Self-Determination Principle to Jews.

"I sincerely hope that the Jews are to be included in President Wilson's promise that he would assist the small nationalities to determine their own future and method of living. I am absolutely in favor of these principles as applied to the Jewish people and all other peoples who are oppressed and persecuted.

For Congress Resolution.

"Finally, let me say, I am in favor of the passage by Congress of an appropriate resolution containing the ideals above outlined."

(Signed)   "HAROLD KNUTSON."

By Representative Carl E. Mapes,
Of Michigan.

Majority of Jews Favorably Inclined.

"In the determination of a question which relates so distinctly to a certain race and affects its vital interests to such an extent as the Zionist movement does the Jewish race, the wishes of the people of that race ought to be given paramount consideration. My information is that the great majority of the Jews everywhere favor the establishment of a Jewish nation in Palestine as advocated by the Zionists. That does not mean, as I understand it, that they all desire to return to Palestine and become citizens of the proposed Jewish state, but rather that an opportunity may be given to those Jews who are oppressed or who may for any reason desire to do so to return to Palestine and become citizens of a country governed by members of their own race and that their people may once again have a distinct national existence. Every sentiment and feeling of justice to the Jewish race leads one to favor the accomplishment of that purpose.

Will Support Congress Resolution.

"I am, therefore, glad to enroll myself as one in accord with the spirit of the declaration of the British government favoring the establishment in Palestine of a National Home for the Jewish people in accordance with the Zionist movement and I should be glad to support a resolution of similar import by the Congress of the United States."   (Signed)   "CARL E. MAPES."

By Representative **Clarence B. Miller,**
Of Minnesota.

"I have all along been convinced that the question of building a Jewish State in Palestine should be decided by the wishes of the Jews of the world. If the Jews desire to build a big Jewish State in Palestine, as its center, I am for the movement.

Will be Guided by Decision of Jews.

"A great Jewish nation established in the ancient home of the Jews, would in the course of reasonable time become one of the powerful nations of the world, making to the world a great contribution of literature, science, and economics. Personally, I should very much desire to see such a nation established. A strong nation, located there, would mark an end to Mohammedism and its like, and establish religious and economic feeling in that old quarter of the world. International political results would be important. I believe the other nations of the world would greet such a new Jewish nation in an unusually friendly spirit."

Social, Economic and Religious Benefits of Jewish Restoration.

(Signed)   "CLARENCE B. MILLER."

By Representative Thomas D. Schall,
Of Minnesota.

Jewish Civilization Resisted Surrounding Ignorance and Barbarism.

"Being full of my four weeks' experience with the American Forces at the Front, where I met with hundreds and hundreds of Jews, and realized the tremendous enthusiasm with which they are throughout the American line, fighting the world's battle, I am in proper tune to harmonize with the international anthem welling up in praise of this long-delayed justice.

"For more than twenty centuries, the Jew has been persecuted because he feared the wrath of God more than that of man and loved truth more than life. They are a people martyred for principle, because they hope to wear out the power to inflict by patient endurance of suffering. The history of their misery would fill volumes. All Europe is stained with their blood. If patient suffering ennobles, the Jew is without peer, and has earned the chosen vessel of national heritage.

"Back through all ages along the path of civilization the Jew has shed a continuous light. When barbaric darkness settled over the world, the Jew retained his former civilization. The Jews were a strong factor in the golden age of Egypt, Greece, Rome, and when ignorance and superstition came and swept all Europe back centuries, the Jew resisted and continues to resist.

"When kings could not write their names, and the monks of the West were spelling out their litanies, the Jews were lecturing on scientific, political and ethical subjects. The Jewish doctors were studying natural laws and laying the foundation of our present system of medicine. Their universities were unrivalled and the revival of learning is due to the influence of the Jew more than to any other cause.

Let the Jew Turn His Face Toward Jerusalem.

"The God, Jehovah, has continued to flame like a sun in the forehead of modern civilization. Among the nations of the earth, Jehovah yet rules, who ages ago fixed the limit of Israel's bondage in Egypt.

"When the fulness of time was come, the iron gates swung under the touch of the Death Angel's hand, and Israel went forth to freedom. When his hour struck,

134

the captive in Babylon turned his face toward Jerusalem. It will be so again. Soon, as, in the glow of the evolution of man, his heart gradually refines and softens, and life becomes broader, fuller and richer, there will be a coming together of those yet unreconciled. 'Each advancing from his shadows into a space made beautiful with the radiance of Charity.' When the world is safe for Democracy, will the curtain fall on the tragedy of the Wandering Jew, and justice and right shall have prevailed."

(Signed)   "THOMAS D. SCHALL."

By Representative Halvor Steenerson, Of Minnesota.

"I entirely approve the British declaration of November 2, 1917, which reads as follows:

Believes in Rule by the Majority.

" 'His Majesty's Government views with favor the establishment in Palestine of a National Home for the Jewish people and will use its best endeavors to facilitate the achievement of this object, *it being clearly understood that nothing shall be done which may prejudice the civil and religious rights of non-Jewish communities in Palestine, or the rights and political status enjoyed by Jews in any other country,*' I submit that the qualifying words I have underscored so limit its meaning that it affords no support to the contention that it favors the establishment of an *independent Jewish nation* in Palestine. Within these limitations I sympathize with and favor the efforts of Jewish people to establish a Homeland or centre in that country. Under the free democratic institutions, which are to be established there, they can, if sufficiently numerous and united politically, control the affairs and destinies of the country. In other words, they will enjoy the same privileges in Palestine as American citizens do in the United States, and no one, I take it, asks or expects more than that."

(Signed)   "HALVOR STEENERSON."

135

By Representative Thomas Upton Sisson,
Of Mississippi.

Favors Home in Palestine.

"I state without hesitation that my sympathy has always been with the Jew in the lands in which he has been denied equal citizenship and equal rights with all other citizens.

"I favor the establishment in Palestine of a home for all Jews of all the lands of the world where the Jews are oppressed where they can work out their own destiny, practise their own religion and entertain their own views. I believe with Thomas Jefferson that the government should have nothing to do with men's religion. I look with horror upon the persecution of the Jew throughout the world on account of his religion and this has been the chief reason for the Jewish persecution in all lands.

Pledges Support.

"I also would cheerfully support an appropriate Constitutional resolution in Congress, favoring the establishment in Palestine of a Jewish National Centre, provided all the interests of all the parties concerned and interested in lands and property in Palestine were observed.

"There can be no objection to the effort of the Jewish people throughout the world to establish a national home in Palestine. If they desire to assume a position as a nation and are able to acquire proper control of a sufficient amount of territory, I think that they should be given this opportunity, provided in so doing, they do not interfere with or trespass upon the rights of others.

Jewish History One of Enterprise and Accomplishment.

"The history of the Jewish race is a history, as a rule, of noble enterprises and great accomplishments. In every intellectual field the Jew has rivalled all races and people. In music, in science, in law and oratory they have been the equal of any people on earth and in religion they have furnished the foundation for all the religions of Christendom.

"I want to assure you, and, through you, all the Jews throughout the world that they have my entire sympathy in the oppression which they have received in so many lands." (Signed) "T. U. Sisson."

By Representative Charles F. Booher,
Of Missouri.

"I have read with a great deal of pleasure the Declarations of England, France, and Italy, on the Zionist question. These declarations seems to voice the sentiment that should, to my mind, be shared by every liberty loving citizen of this country. If the proposition is practical, and according to recent events it would seem to be, to establish a Jewish country with the capital city at Jerusalem, I certainly would favor such a proposition and any action that the United States might take in bringing this to a happy conclusion.

"To give the Jews of the world a homeland, a flag, and a government of their own is a beautiful thought, and I will in my humble way help all I can to its realization."

(Signed) "CHAS. F. BOOHER."

All Liberty-Lovers should Indorse.

Will Help Re-establishment.

By Representative **William P. Borland,**
Of Missouri.

Lofty Ideals of Zionists.

"The aspirations of the Jewish people for a home in the ancient land of Judah—the land which God gave to their father Abraham—is perfectly understandable. It enlists my deepest sympathy by the fine quality of the intent which underlies it. No sordid sense, no mercenary motive, dictates this desire, for the Jews have done well in a material way in every land in which their fortunes have been cast. They have no hope of riches in a return to the worn land of Palestine. The Return means, in truth, to many of them, a sacrifice of place and power and possessions.

No Political Ambitions.

"Neither can they gratify a purely political ambition. Jews now sit at the council table of the greatest nations on the globe. They have a hand in ruling the world. Their political power cannot be increased by their organization into a separate state. A Jewish state could never become so powerful as to dominate world politics, for if it should attain that eminence, it would inevitably band all nations into a league against it to accomplish its limitations.

Restoration Would Perpetuate Higher Ideals.

"The hope of the Jews in the erection of a Jewish state upon the sacred soil is entirely religious and ethical. Such a venture would mean a guarantee of the perpetuation of the ideals for which they have suffered and struggled through the centuries. A Jewish commonwealth would be a haven and a shelter for Jews who might be oppressed in any land. It would be a strong factor for better social conditions, for religious and racial toleration and for world peace. To it, Jews would bring back the intellectual spoils of the world. Its literature, its art, its industry, its statescraft, would be the richest and fullest of all time. Such a land ought to be a veritable garden—the intellectual and artistic gymnasium of a newer and better world."

(Signed) "Wm. P. Borland."

**By Representative Champ Clark,
Of Missouri.**

"For many years I have been very much interested in the Jews. I have no better friends than they are. I am in favor of the Zionist movement. It has seemed to me for a long time that the civilized nations of the earth ought to take the Turks by the neck and throw them over into Asia where they belong. One of the strangest facts in all history to me is that the very rich Jews haven't caught the Sultan on the hip long ago, and made him release Palestine to them.

Movement Will Free Palestine from Turk.

"I am very much in favor of Palestine being erected into an independent state. I do not know enough about the physical formation of Palestine and the climatic conditions to know whether it can be made to support a large population or not; but however that may be, the experiment is certainly well worth trying. I think we ought to help along in the matter."

Experiment Well Worth While.

(Signed)   "Champ Clark."

By Representative Leonidas C. Dyer,
Of Missouri.

Speaker of the House of Representatives.

British Declaration Safeguards Jews in and out of Palestine.

"I approve of the official declarations of England, France, and Italy, as to the establishment of a home for the Jewish people in Palestine. I favor it not only because it contemplates returning to the wandering people of Israel their ancient home, but for the reason that it declares for equality in civil and political rights for the Jewish people in whatever lands they may choose to dwell. This being a War for universal liberty and justice among all the peoples of the world, I recall the important historical struggles of the Jewish people for these very things, and all they have done through the centuries they have been scattered. No reader of the Old Testament can forget that their form of government was one which most nearly resembled our own. That brings to mind the fact that our very Government, formulated as it was by the Pilgrim fathers, comes almost directly out of the Bible, which the Jewish people have given to the world. The Pilgrim fathers, who are the makers of this nation, lived by the light of the Jewish Bible.

Founders of Our Nation Lived by the Light of Jewish Law.

President's Self-Determination Policy Should Apply to Jews.

"The United States Government, speaking through its Executive, has said time and again that it is in favor of self-determination of small nationalities. I take it that this includes the Jewish nation. I am most certainly in favor of the United States Government making an official declaration endorsing what our Allies, Great Britain, France, and Italy, have already declared publicly, urging the establishment of a homeland for the Jewish people in Palestine.

Jewish National Laws Corner-Stone of Our Civilization.

"My special reason for desiring to see the Jewish people restored to nationhood in their own homeland of Palestine, is that the world owes Jewish people a debt of gratitude. They have laid the corner stone of our civilization in the Ten Commandments, in the ethics of the Hebrew prophets, in the wise legislation of Moses, the greatest of law givers, and in planting the ideals by which the world has tried to live. During these stirring times I cannot help thinking of Isaiah and the lofty ideals of peace on earth that he preached. Then too, when we turn to the fields of art, of science and of literature, we find Jews making some of the most important contributions.

"Our own beloved country owes much to the Jewish America's people from its earliest history to this day. With the Debt to men who accompanied Columbus to these shores, there Jews. were Jews. In all the early struggles of the colonies Jews did their part. In the Revolutionary War there were Jewish fighters. Jewish financiers helped finance the War without asking for the return of the moneys which they loaned to the Government. In the Civil War Jews did yeoman service in the ranks as well as in important offices. And if we turn to our own time, we find the Jewish people giving their share, and more, of the men who fight under the Stars and Stripes. As I scan the casualty lists from day to day, I find the names of Jewish boys who have given their lives, or who have been broken in body, that the United States may succeed in this War. Financially, whether the Government solicits loans, whether the Red Cross asks for contributions, or whether it be the Y. M. C. A., the Knights of Columbus, etc., who ask for money to do War work, the Jewish people are among the first to respond and do always more than their share. For these and many more reasons I hope soon to see the day when the Jewish people will again till the soil of their ancestral home so that they may again proclaim to the world the ideals which are so sorely needed by harassed mankind."

(Signed)   "L. C. DYER."

By Representative Walter L. Hensley,
Of Missouri.

"I am heartily in favor of the British declaration for Embody the re-establishment of the Jewish homeland in Pales- Jewish tine, and hope that appropriate action will be taken by a State. the democratic governments to effect the practical consummation of the Zionist movement."

(Signed)   "W. L. HENSLEY."

141

By Representative Milton A. Romjue,
Of Missouri.

Expects
Approval.

"As I see the matter now, the return of your people to Palestine would meet with quite a hearty approval, I am quite sure."   (Signed)   "MILTON A. ROMJUE."

By Representative Jeanette Rankin,
Of Montana.

Expects
Abolition of
Restric-
tions.

"That the Jews should have a land in which they can live fully and freely, without the repressions they have suffered at the hands of almost every nation in the old world with whom they have sought a home is a matter not of philanthropy but of justice. And it is to be expected that after the war we shall witness the abolition of these unfair restrictions and the establishment of the right of Jews to practice their religion freely, to engage in business and to receive an education, to be citizens and voters, and to enjoy all the fundamental rights of human beings living in a highly organized society.

Turkish
Oppression
Ended.

"These rights can and must be guaranteed to the Jews in Palestine. Toleration of national injustice is no longer good form. The heavy tribute which the Turks have always exacted from the Jews, in return for which the Jews were allowed to establish very limited educational and industrial enterprises that were in constant jeopardy of destruction and oppression is a thing of the past. The great nations of the world that are fighting for democracy and justice have recognized this, and assistance in securing justice to the Jews has been pledged.

"The great labor organizations in America, in France, in Great Britain, have all urged the establishment of Palestine as a free and democratic nation in which the Jews may develop their own cultural and economic institutions. And Mr. Arthur Henderson, Labor Member of the House of Commons of Great Britain, was not speaking for himself alone when he said last December: "The British Labour movement has included among its war aims a demand that the Jews of all countries, great and small, shall enjoy the elementary rights of tolerance, freedom of residence and travel, and equal

142

citizenship that ought to be extended to all inhabitants of every nation; and it has so declared its belief that it would be practicable by agreement among all the nations to set Palestine free from the harsh and oppressive government of the Turk, in order that the country may form a Free State, under international guarantee, where the Jewish people may work out their own salvation free from interference by those of alien race and religion.

Labor Supports Declaration.

"If these rights can be guaranteed to the Jews in Palestine, then those Jews who desire to go back to the land of their fathers to live a free, unrestricted Jewish life, to speak Hebrew, to develop their own educational and economic systems, their own literature, their own industrial and cultural institutions, should be allowed to do so. And those Jews in every country in the world, who do not care to go back to Palestine, should nevertheless enjoy the consciousness that in Palestine they have a centre of Jewish culture upon which they may rely for the development of the Jewish race.

Favors Establishment of Jews in Palestine.

"By its geographical position, Palestine stands as a gateway between the eastern and western worlds. It is, therefore, peculiarly susceptible to commercial exploitation by the more powerful nations.

"But Palestine must not be a project for financial exploitation. Like the other small nations for whose rights we are fighting, Palestine must stand free and independent, respected by the nations of the world for the intelligence and earnestness of its endeavor and for the contributions it will make to the development of world civilization.

"The time is at hand to congratulate the Jews upon the imminent realization of their dream of centuries, and to help them to re-establish themselves in their old home, to the end that economic and cultural benefits may redound to themselves and to the world."

Realization Imminent.

(Signed)   "JEANETTE RANKIN."

By Representative Moses P. Kinkaid,
Of Nebraska.

Favors a
National
Home.   "I will say the proposal to establish a National Home in Palestine for the Jewish people meets with my hearty approval."   (Signed)   "M. P. Kinkaid."

By Representative Charles C. Lobeck,
Of Nebraska.

Palestine
Protectorate
Solves
Jewish
Problem.   "I certainly sympathize with the object to establish a Jewish Homeland in Palestine. I am certain that if the opportunity is given to the people of the Jewish faith to occupy Palestine under some kind of a Protectorate of the United States, Great Britain, France, and Italy, it would be solving satisfactorily the problem that has occupied the minds of all religious faiths.

World to
Support
Palestine
Government.   "I am sure nothing would please me more than to learn and know that Palestine, the home of ancient, sacred history—so dear to all peoples of every faith—would be restored in some degree to its ancient position among the official nations of the world. I feel sure that a Government in Palestine, founded on the principles of righteousness, will have the support of the peoples of the world and that Palestine will come into its own and the prophesies of its greatness by prophets of old will be fully fulfilled."   (Signed)   "C. C. Lobeck."

**By Representative Charles H. Sloan,
Of Nebraska.**

"With all the debit of blood and treasure chargeable to this great war, there are many counterveiling credits which we hope will show a large balance in favor of righteousness and human progress. Among the achievements now in prospect is the realization of the Jewish National aspiration for the recovery of their ancient domain for habitation and control.

Restoration One of Compensations for War.

"There is that in their long treasured purpose, undaunted by difficulties and unweakened by persecution, which challenges our admiration, commands our interest and commends our support.

"The race which in that elder day gave us the jurisprudence of Moses, the poetry of David, the eloquence of Isaiah, the philosophy of Solomon and the valor of militant leaders from Joshua to the Maccabees, and whose members in this later day credit our professions, lead in finance, adorn our literature and constitute much of the world's best citizenship, may well, under suitable recognition and encouragement of the Allied powers, repopulate the land of their fathers, and with full scope for their governmental genius, establish and maintain a government which will be a creditable world factor.

Favors Recognition of Zionism.

"I favor American recognition and encouragement of ZIONISM and shall support all well considered action for its accomplishment."

(Signed)   "CHARLES H. SLOAN."

By Representative Dan V. Stephens,
Of Nebraska.

Free Birth-
place of
Christianity
from Turk
and Restore
Homeland
to Jews.

"The whole civilized Christian world must be gratified with the progress which has been made by the Allied forces toward freeing the Holy Land from the rule of the Turk. It is the homeland of the Jews, and the seat of the birth of Christianity. Nothing has happened in this great war more sentimentally pleasing than the prospect created by the splendid victories of the British Army over the Turks, of restoring to the Jewish people their homeland and sacred shrines.

"I am heartily in accord with the policy set forth by the Allied governments for the future autonomous government of the Holy Land by the people and for the people who live there."

(Signed)   "DAN V. STEPHENS."

By Representative Sherman E. Burroughs,
Of New Hampshire.

"I have entirely approved of the recent declarations made by England, France and Italy on the Zionist question. *In Favor of Declaration.*

"I am also much in favor of similar action on the part of the United States Government. I hope such action may be taken in the near future. *Similar Action By Government.*

"I would certainly favor the adoption of a proper resolution by Congress in favor of the establishment in Palestine of a national Jewish center. *Resolution By Congress.*

"My principal reason for this position is that such action recognizes the Jews as a distinct nationality, and also recognizes the Jewish claim to Palestine. Both of these claims to my mind, are just, and their recognition at this time would be, in my opinion, especially appropriate when this nation and its Allies are engaged in a great war of liberation in which oppressed nationalities are to find deliverance. *Just Claims of Jews to Nationality and to Palestine.*

"I deeply sympathize with the aspirations of the Jewish people, maintained for so many centuries, to establish again a home in Palestine. It may well be that the great genius of this race will again be able to give to the world a brilliant and distinctive civilization. The remarkable combination of qualities that go to make up the Jewish mind, enabled it for many centuries in Palestine to produce an almost unbroken series of statesmen, soldiers, judges, poets, prophets and seers, thinkers and leaders, who have, for all time, left their impress upon the world. The Jewish mind is very tenacious and persists after all the powerful empires that overran that land have been overthrown and almost forgotten. *For Jewish Re-establishment.*

"You may be sure that I shall do everything that is within my power to do, to promote the success of the movement you represent, and I trust that I may have an early opportunity to vote for a resolution in Congress in line with the British Declaration." *Will Vote For Resolution.*

(Signed)   "SHERMAN E. BURROUGHS."

147

By Representative Isaac Bachrach,
Of New Jersey.

Loyalty to Judaism Demands Indorsement of Zionism. "In the words of the great leader, Max Nordau, 'the period of rhetoric is over, the hour of deeds is approaching.' Every Jew be he statesman or tradesman, professional or layman, whatever his calling in life may be, who regards the declaration of Great Britain on November 2, 1918, namely:

" 'As viewing with favor the establishment in Palestine of a national home for the Jewish people, etc.,' with a feeling short of reverence, and who does not give it his full-hearted support is not a loyal Jew. He is to Judaism, its principles and ideals, what that type of American citizenship is to America, its hopes and aspirations, who with one hand waves the stars and stripes and with the other is grabbing all the excess profits he can in his dealings with Uncle Sam.

Pittsburgh Resolution and Basle Program Faithful to Principles of Judaism. "What figure or more beautiful illustration of faithful adherence to principle can be found than in the resolution adopted at the last Zionist Convention held in Pittsburgh which resolved:

"Therefore we desire to affirm anew the principles which have guided the Zionist Movement since its inception, and which were the foundations laid down by law givers and prophets for the ancient Jewish state and were the inspiration of the living Jewish law embodied in the traditions of two thousand years of exile.

"Thus re-pledging itself to the object of Zionism as defined at the first Zionist Congress held at Basle, in 1896, to wit:

" 'The establishment of a publicly recognized, legally secured homeland for the Jewish people in Palestine.'

Zionist Dream Realized. "Yes.—No longer is the 'publicly recognized and legally secured home for the Jewish people in Palestine' a mere dream or fantasy. The declaration of Great Britain, as we all know, has been received with equal favor by Italy, France, and all Allied democratic Nations. A Jewish National home, no longer a dream, is a reality; no longer a fantasy, is an international fact.

Founders and adherents to the Congress at Basle, well
may you be proud of your accomplishments.

"Righteousness, justice and democracy, in its finest _{Will Sup-}
and broadest exemplifications, the foundation of Jewish _{port in}
traditions and national life, finds anew, as ever before, _{Congress.}
a champion in glorious, unselfish and idealistic America.
That equal opportunity; that government shall derive its
power by the consent of those governed; that the rule of
right shall forever supplant the rule of might; are the
objects of America's intervention in this great conflict.
As a member of Congress I shall of course lend every
effort for the accomplishment of those principles. Every
other cause must abide the one great yearning which
every American possesses—Victory. To the forces of
Zionism I shall consider it a privilege to render whatever service I can."

(Signed)   "ISAAC BACHRACH."

**By Representative William J. Browning,
Of New Jersey.**

"It is my pleasure to state to you that I am whole- _{One of}
heartedly in favor of the development of the plan to _{Desired}
establish a Jewish Homeland in Palestine. It will be _{Fruitions}
one of the desired fruitions of the world war." _{of War.}

(Signed)   "WM. J. BROWNING."

By Representative Edward W. Gray,
Of New Jersey.

Declarations Indorsed.

"It seems to me that every broad-minded American will find his views on Zionist aspirations well expressed in the words of the Honorable Arthur J. Balfour. As the views expressed by the representatives of the French and Italian governments coincide with those of Mr. Balfour, officially expressed for the British Government, it would seem proper to assume that these are also the views of the Government of the United States. I am free to say that they have my personal endorsement.

Time For National Establishment.

"In the readjustment of the world's affairs that is now going on, the outline of which shall more clearly be seen when the great war is ended, would not a national establishment of the Jewish race be an ideal concomitant of this readjustment? The Jewish people have maintained their racial integrity through many centuries and under many different flags. It would logically appear that the time has come when they should have a flag of their own, and should this desired result be accomplished, it will in nowise detract from the glory of the Jewish accomplishment in the past nor necessarily diminish the possibilities of Jewish accomplishment in the future.

Favors Action By Our Government.

"In the three European nations that have officially expressed themselves in favor of the establishment of a national home for the Jews in Palestine, are found the best expressions of democracy in Europe. Great Britain and Italy are under a monarchical form of government, while France is a republic. In the great republic of the United States, therefore, in which modern democracy found its first foundation and where liberality of view has its widest scope, it is fully to be expected that the Government will follow in line with the British Declaration and move sincerely and earnestly toward its realization. I shall gladly favor the adoption of an appropriate resolution in Congress for the establishment in Palestine of a Jewish national center.

Advises Wide Publicity.

"I might say in addition that the efforts of the nations that are favorable to the project in view must to a great extent depend upon the wishes of the Jewish people themselves. The more widely and earnestly they make known their desire for national unity, the more prompt will be the international response. As I suggested above, the time seems to be as ideal, as the project is itself, for this, one of the most historic of all the peoples of the earth, to re-establish themselves on a national basis in the land where they originated."

(Signed) "E. W. GRAY."

By Representative Elijah C. Hutchinson,
Of New Jersey.

"I am a strong adherent of the original Zionist formula urging a 'legally secured and publicly recognized home for the Jews in Palestine.' The so-called Balfour declaration furnished this legal assurance and the almost universal acceptance of this official announcement supplied it with public recognition. The Basle program is thus growing into an actuality before our very eyes. Zionism has passed the stage of being a mere theory or a debatable matter—it is a fact, one to be reckoned with. *Zionism no Longer Debatable.*

"It has afforded me much pleasure to see this Jewish national movement growing stronger and more entrenched from day to day until it went 'over the top' through the British declaration in its favor. I cannot conceive how any true and loyal American citizen, or anyone who is imbued with the just cause of this war, can rightly refrain from supporting Zionism now that it had been put forward by our allies as one of their aims. France, Italy, Serbia, Belgium, and all the rest have officially recognized and indorsed the British declaration. To oppose it now would be antagonizing the aims of democracy against autocracy. *Anti-Zionists are Champions of Autocracy.*

"I do not believe it would be necessary to obtain any action by Congress favoring the British declaration. The Allies and our Executive Department will keep their solemn promise without any further reminders. However, should such action be required, in order to safeguard the realization of Zionism, I would be glad to support a Zionist resolution in the Congress of the United States." *Support Congress Resolution if Necessary.*

(Signed) "E. C. HUTCHINSON."

By Representative Frederick R. Lehlbach,
Of New Jersey.

Favors
Declaration
by Gov-
ernment.

"The declaration by the British Government 'viewing with favor the establishment in Palestine of a national home for the Jewish people' and expressing its willingness 'to facilitate the achievement of this object' is in accord with the present-day universal sympathy with national aspirations of weaker peoples. I trust that the government of the United States will join the French and Italian governments in their indorsements of this Declaration, and I will be glad to assist in causing such action to be taken.

Success
Depends on
Jewish
Immigration.

"The practical value of such a movement will, however, depend upon the attitude toward it of the great masses of Jews throughout the world. The mere establishment of a Jewish governmental machine in Palestine will be of little significance unless the Hebrew race, in appreciable numbers, will in fact make this land their home."

(Signed) "Frederick R. Lehlbach."

By Representative John R. Ramsey,
Of New Jersey.

Favors Self-
Determina-
tion for
Small
Nations.

"I should use my very best endeavors to help the Jews in every possible way. I am in favor of anything which is helpful to any small nationality, in giving it an opportunity to develop in its own historic ways and manners. This necessarily includes the Jews. From the cursory examination that I have made of the British, French and Italian official declarations in favor of a Jewish homeland in Palestine, I should be rather inclined to take the same attitude as was taken by these, our allies. I would furthermore be in favor of our Government taking similar action at such time when it would appear advisable to every one concerned.

Foresees
no Reason
for Opposi-
tion.

"I feel certain that should an appropriate resolution be introduced into Congress regarding the matter of a Jewish homeland in Palestine, I should give it the best consideration and attention on my part with a view of doing justice to the Jewish people all over the world. As I see it now, I can imagine no reason why I should be inclined to vote against such resolution."

(Signed) "John R. Ramsey."

By Representative John F. Carew,
Of New York.

"I would be glad to see the objects of the Zionist Indorses movement accomplished in the way proposed by the Zionism. leaders of that ideal, and the Jewish problem solved along the lines indicated by the British Declaration."

(Signed) "JOHN F. CAREW."

By Representattive Walter M. Chandler,
Of New York.*

National Aspirations of Jews.

"The Zionist movement has many ardent advocates and able supporters among Jews and Gentiles throughout the earth. The great world struggle has given a powerful impetus to this movement. Besides, the national idea and the religious self-consciousness of the Hebrew race in all ages have been seeds awaiting ripening for such an event. It has been truly said that 'since the destruction of the second temple by Titus, since the dispersion of the Jews throughout the world, this ancient people has not ceased to long fervently for a return to the lost land of their fathers nor to entertain for it a determined hope.'

Overcoming Possible Obstacles.

"The obstacles to this new plan of erecting an independent Jewish State in Palestine are many, but not insuperable. The British Government and her allies propose to guarantee to the Jews the return of the territory of their ancient Jewish fatherland. The two great essential elements of such an enterprise are in existence—a country without a people and a people without a country.

Tide of Immigration already Flowing towards Palestine.

"Palestine is about the size of the State of Vermont, and has a present population of about 600,000 souls. There are about 14,000,000 Jews in the world. If half this number were to return to the ancient home of their race, the country could not well maintain them, but the present Zionist movement does not contemplate such an exodus of Jews from their present homes. According to a conservative estimate, the territory of Palestine could easily maintain a population of four and one-half millions of people. A successful culmination of this movement would probably realize an emigration of that number from other lands, as the innate love of the average Jew for the cradle land of his race, coupled with glorious and thrilling memories of long ago, and the hard lot of misery and grinding toil now endured by many of them in different parts of the world, would be a powerful incentive to join the new settlements in the East. The tide of emigration is already beginning to flow that way.

154

"There is no reason from a physical viewpoint why Jerusalem and the surrounding country should not become the seat of a prosperous and successful Jewish State. The popular notion that Palestine is a barren country, not capable of yielding rich harvests, is a mistaken one. Its appearance is barren only during the dry season, when the grasses which cover the greater part of it are dried up, and the herdsmen retire with their flocks of sheep and goats to the loftier mountains. The alluvial lowland to the sound of Mount Carmel is as fruitful as ever, and it only needs an honest and vigorous administration to restore Palestine to its former fruitful condition. *[Popular Conception of Land's Infertility Erroneous.]*

"An enlightened political management would not only rekindle the olden Jewish love of agriculture, but would revive the ancient glories of Phoenician commerce through the ports of Acre and Jaffa, which would give an outlet to all the world. *[Agricultural and Commercial Possibilities.]*

"All the spiritual and intellectual elements would certainly be present in the building and perpetuating of a new Jewish commonwealth in Palestine. The Bible and the Talmud would again be their religious guides and the charters of their freedom. A Maccabaean soldiery would again defend their national frontiers. A Jerusalem parliament would be heard to echo the splendid eloquence of new Disraelis, Gambettas, and Castelars. Some new Josephus would record the growth of the expanding State, and the melodies of Mendelssohn and Meyerbeer would cheer and sanctify the domestic circles of happy Jewish homes. Such a commonwealth, kingdom or republic, is a consummation most devoutly to be wished, if Jewish genius and civilization are not to be lost, as is now feared, in the maelstrom of war and in the readjustment of the boundaries of States and the realignment of races. *[Preserve Jewish Civilization and Genius by Embodying Ideals in a State.]*

"Why should not the nations of the earth join in such an enterprise, if the Jews desire it? Every kingdom of the earth has tried its hand at exterminating them and has failed. Why should they not now change the program for awhile and extend to the patriarch of the tribes, the old man of the centuries, a kindly and helping hand? England will turn Palestine over to the Jewish people. *[Let Nations Aid Zionism.]*

The Christian nations of the globe could place their fleets for transportation at the disposal of honest, struggling Jews who desire to link their lives and fortunes to the land of their fathers and with the early memories of their race.

Action by Executive and Congress.

"I am perfectly in accord with the Declaration made by England, France and Italy, and believe that our own Government should follow suit. Should an appropriate resolution come up for consideration in Congress, I shall consider it my duty to support it."

(Signed)   "WALTER M. CHANDLER."

---

*Representative Chandler published this statement, as part of his speech, in the *Congressional Record*, on May 13, 1918, headed "The Zionist Movement."

By Representative W. E. Cleary,
Of New York.

"In a question involving the very life of an entire nation, of the very historic existence of a people, it is wise and just to be guided by the wishes of that nation, expressed directly or indirectly. The question, therefore, resolves itself into this: Do the Jewish people favor Zionism? Are they in hearty sympathy with this Hebraic nationalistic tendency? The answer to this is very apparent to any one who has had the slightest acquaintance with the Jews. In recent years, especially, the Jews of the world in general, and those of America in particular, have expressed their desires and aspirations for Zionism in tones and acts unmistakable. I am informed that the Jewish press, the great Jewish readers, the various Jewish orders and organizations are practically unanimous in their heartiest approval and co-operation to the end that justice be done to the Jewish nation along the lines indicated by the British Declaration and by the platform of the Zionist Organization. *Jews Almost Unanimous for Palestine.*

"A nation may, in many respects, be compared and judged like an individual. It is the will of the individual which is the uppermost fact in directing him to his success, and so it is the strong united will of a nation which is solely responsible in bringing national success to that people. This great war happened to be the vehicle on which the Jewish Land, the Jewish Government, will be ushered into the world; but it may be safely assumed that under any and all conditions, disregarding the importance of this war, the Jews would finally have emerged the victors in their ambitions and hopes, and Palestine would eventually have become a Jewish State. This is the course of historic events, and no fatalistic principles would have stood in its way. *Realization Certain.*

"To help in the accomplishing of this great purpose, I shall give my aid unstintingly, and afford assistance, if need be, as a member of the great American Congress, and know that I shall be one of a great majority. It is pleasing to me to be in position to render such assistance." *Promises Help.*

(Signed)   "W. E. CLEARY."

157

**By Representative S. Wallace Dempsey,
Of New York.**

Jewish
Restoration
Source of
Inspiration
to Near-
East.

"From the time of the Crusades, the nations of Western Europe have dreamed of rescuing Palestine from the hands of men opposed to the Christian religion and of re-establishing the Jews in their ancient home. What was undertaken in a romantic and desultory way by Richard of England and his associates, seven hundred years ago, has held the admiration of the world for that long period. What was then attempted is, to-day, being accomplished and its importance is not quite fully realized owing to the magnitude of the Great War in Western Europe. The regaining of the Holy Land is, however, one of the memorable historical events of all time. It should naturally lead to the re-settlement of the country by the Jews, from all the countries of the world. This would naturally result in the re-establishment of the Jews as a Nation and they, with their progressiveness and energy, would serve as an example and inspiration to the people of all the nearby lands of the East."

(Signed)   "S. WALLACE DEMPSEY."

The American War Congress and Zionism

By Representative Jerome F. Donovan,
Of New York.

"In the same sense as one's domicile is, in law, not necessarily changed by a mere change of residence, but continues to be the spot which one most truly regards as his home, Palestine has at all times, and still continues to be, the domicile of millions of Jews, who have never ceased to yearn and pray for their return to the sacred soil of their fathers. These Jews have never, for a moment, renounced their first and fundamental allegiance to that country. Their noblest desire is there to carry on their distinctive genius, the great and thrice-blessed culture of the Jewish people. They have indeed constituted, and still continue to constitute the Jewish people, as distinguished from the other peoples of the earth. The Age-long denial to them of their home-land has not only constituted a cruel and inhuman tragedy to the Jewish people, but has also constituted a menace to the harmony of the cultures of the world, for no national culture can forever continue to survive banishment, and the world will never cease to wonder how the Jewish genius has survived it so long.

"The highest duty of an individual is to be true to himself—to the innermost longings of his soul. But before this becomes his duty, it must become his privilege. A man should have the right to be true to himself. Only after he has acquired this right may we look for the performance of this duty.

"I speak of this principle as bearing on the relation of the subject under discussion, to the duty of patriotism. the most pressing duty of the hour. The Jew, upon freely adopting America, must be true to America. As soon as he is endowed with all the rights of American citizenship, he must be true to himself as an American citizen. He owes America what every other American owes it; a single-hearted and all absorbing devotion. His spirt must be purely American. He must draw upon and contribute to the American genius—a genius which, however lavishly it may draw from the ancient genius of the Jewish people, is, nevertheless, no other genius but its

Palestine always Jewish Home.

Diaspora Menace to Culture.

For True Self-Expression a People Need a Home.

own.   The same is true, of course, of the Englishman,
the Frenchman, the Italian or the member of any other
nationality, who of his own free will and accord adopts
America as his home.   There is only this difference as
regards outward circumstances.   The Frenchman who
does not adopt America, can still be true to himself, by
being true to France.   Likewise, largely as to the other
nationalities.   The Jew, who desires to remain a Jew,
however, is denied this privilege, and is therefore unable
to exercise his highest duty.   His home denied to him, he
perforce adopts this or that country, and the very element
of compulsion in this adoption negatives the existence
of the equality of rights, with its inevitable corollary, the
equality of duties.

National Self-Expression most Precious Gift.

"The unescapable logic of the foregoing is that the
Jew, who has not spontaneously adopted this or any
other country, as his home—to whom Palestine alone is
domicile and home-land, ought to be afforded ample
opportunity to give expression to his highest self by becoming a citizen of Palestine.   That large or small
remnant of Jews, as the case may be, constituting in a
comparative sense the Jewish people, should no longer
be denied the very thing that is most worth while in
human life.

Realization of Zionist Aspirations Will Benefit World.

"Would not the world at large be the loser for crimi-
nally failing to avail itself of this, the greatest occasion
for reconstruction that it has ever had by restoring free
and fair play to a genius, a culture, a national soul, to
which it owes the spiritual aspect, the highest aspect of
its civilization?

America Signatory in Spirit.

"My views of the British declarations are, therefore,
self-evident, and I am sure that the United States is, in
spirit signatory thereto, even as are the French and
Italian governments.   As a member of Congress I shall
most heartily join in the adoption, at the first opportune
moment, of an appropriate resolution in precise conformity to this epochal declaration."

(Signed)   "Jerome F. Donovan."

The American War Congress and Zionism

By Representative Benjamin L. Fairchild,
Of New York.

"As an American and a friend of Democracy, I approve to the fullest extent all the declarations made by various Allied Governments, in favor of the establishment of a Jewish home-land in Palestine. It was a very appropriate and wise move on the part of the Allied Governments to make the Zionist ideal one of their chief aims. The sentiments of the American people, frequently and publicly expressed, are unqualifiedly in favor of the re-establishment of Israel's home. I feel it my duty as an American to support this movement which has now become world wide and which is nothing more than the bringing of justice to the Jews, of which they have been deprived for so many hundreds of years. It is indeed a privilege to lend assistance in this direction and I gladly grasp the opportunity to do so. *(Duty as American to Support.)*

"It has always been somewhat surprising how some people misunderstood the Zionist aspirations. I believe it was Justice Brandeis who put the matter very clearly in stating that Zionism was not aiming to bring to Palestine any Jew who is unwilling to go there, nor does Zionism tend to prohibit anyone, Jew or Gentile, from settling in the Holy Land. The ideals of Zionism, in their broad meaning, are the very ideals of the Fathers of our Country. It is surely very fitting that we, this greatest Republic in the new world, should be of material and spiritual assistance in the formation of the Republic of the oldest nation in the old world. We Americans who realize our patriotic duty and who love our institutions and freedom, are peculiarly fit to understand, and to extend the greatest sympathy and assistance to the Jews in many lands who are deprived of all these rights and are striving to possess what is the common gift of the great majority of mankind. *(Ideals of Zionism and Americanism Are One. America to Assist New Republic.)*

"My sympathies in this direction are not merely limited to the official Declarations of the Allied Governments, but they extend to the great Zionist movement in general that has spread with accelerated momentum among the Jews all over the world in the last thirty odd years. *(Unqualified Indorsement of Jewish National Movement.)*

161

Would
Support
Congress
Resolution

"Having these sentiments, it is only logical that I shall do my very best in support of a resolution that may be introduced in Congress incorporating the aims of Zionism. If this purpose was accomplished by President Wilson's declaration in its favor, it may perhaps not be necessary to introduce that resolution. But I am ready at all times to aid the Zionists in every way possible."   (Signed)   "BEN. L. FAIRCHILD."

By Representative Joseph V. Flynn,
Of New York.

Would
Support
Congress
Resolution.

"I desire to state that I have given the matter some thought and am inclined to heartily agree with the declaration of England, France and Italy on the Zionist question. I am in favor of the establishment of a National Home for the Jewish people in their old home in Palestine and will gladly do what I can to bring this consummation about. I would be in favor of action by the United States Government in line with the declaration of the above named powers at whatever time is deemed most appropriate, and if a resolution by Congress should be necessary, I would gladly vote for it.

Movement
Should be
Encouraged.

"The efforts of the Jewish people to establish their national home and work out their own destinies as a race and people should meet with the encouragement of every broad-minded man. It is consistent with the avowed purposes of this nation in the present world war and with the declaration of the President in regard to the rights of small nationalities. This sentiment should be made to apply to all peoples and races who think enough of their own existence and nationality to demand that they be given a right to work out their own traditions and ideals.

Would See
National
Aspirations
Realized.

"When the time comes to finally adjust this question in the world's affairs, as come it must, and when all claims must be considered, I shall expect and hope to see the Jewish people, who have contributed so much to the liberties of mankind through the ages, recognized as a separate, distinct nationality, among the nations of the world, established in their own territory, their future guaranteed, living their own life and history as an integral part of this world's affairs."

(Signed)   "JOSEPH V. FLYNN.

By Representative George B. Francis,
Of New York.

"I agree with the Declaration of Secretary Balfour Liberal regarding the establishment of a Jewish Homeland in Palestine. My view is that if the Jewish people wish to re-establish themselves in Palestine they should have the hearty support of all the liberal-minded people and liberal-minded governments. I do not know what form this support should take, but I have sufficient confidence in the fair-mindedness of the Allies to believe that when they have won this war they will permit the Jewish people to appear at whatever conferences are held for the purpose of restoring world peace, and permit them through their representatives to express their national ambitions, and gladly do everything to enable them to be effectuated."

      (Signed) "GEORGE B. FRANCIS."

By Representative Anthony J. Griffin,
Of New York.

"I welcome the announcement of the intention of the Allied governments to establish in Palestine a National Home for the Jewish race. I do not know whether the purpose is to establish there an autonomous nation, but whatever the intent I feel that the civilized world will acknowledge with joy the proposal to rescue the Holy places of the Christian and Jewish religions from the domination of the unspeakable Turk. A similar declaration as to Armenia would be equally welcome.

"I have many friends among the Jews, and I do not find among them any evidence of either wish or purpose to relinquish their allegiance to the United States of America in order to affiliate themselves with the New Jewish Commonwealth. The Jews who are in the United States are a part of this great nation irrevocably welded into its structure, but there are many members of the race in countries less tolerant and liberal than ours, who would grasp at the opportunity to find rest, peace and happiness in the home of their fathers.

"With this thought in mind I cannot too highly commend the Zionist movement."

      (Signed) "ANTHONY J. GRIFFIN."

By Representative Reuben L. Haskell,
Of New York.

Lofty Ideals of Zionism.

"To me the principle of Zionism, as it is expressed effectually in the British Declaration to the Zionists of England, has a particular attraction because of the lofty principles and high ideals which it brings in its wake. The proposition has assumed world significance.

Will Have Favorable Reaction on Jews.

"I am for the British declaration because I consider it will bring the most desirable result in the development of the democratic ideal, because it will serve to solve one of the great problems of all history, will bring to realization a dream of ages to a people of ages, and because it will develop generally among Jews those qualities and adaptabilities now possessed by the more advanced and progressive Jews even now constituting the great majority. In short, I am for the declaration because of these and many other reasons.

State Will Augment World's Spiritual Treasure.

"The traditions, history and ideals of Palestine make a very strong appeal. When the Jews were the rulers of the land they gave so much to the world, which is indebted to them to this day, that surely this new state will continue to add to the spiritual treasure of humanity as was the case in ancient times.

Would Enlist among Supporters of Cause.

"This is, indeed, an enterprise to be applauded and supported by every one. It will give millions of Jews an opportunity, once again in their history of multitudinous experiences, to demonstrate the wisdom of their laws and customs. I have sympathized with this Zionist movement; in fact, with all movements for the amelioration of the present struggles that still exist after a history of two thousand years. I should, therefore, be glad to be counted among the supporters of the Zionist principle and of the British declaration.

Congress Resolution Would Find Support in Both Houses.

"It is my firm belief that the United States Government should speak unmistakably in this matter as soon as possible by a resolution to Congress in favor of the establishment in Palestine of an independent Jewish National Center. I am confident that such a resolution would receive the hearty support of the representatives of the American people in both houses of Congress."

(Signed) "REUBEN L. HASKELL."

164

The American War Congress and Zionism

By Representative Florello H. LaGuardia,
Of New York.

"I do not approve of the official declarations of England, France and Italy on the Zionist question. Opposes Declaration.

"My reasons for not favoring it, briefly stated, are:

"I do not believe that it is to the interest of the Jews or the world to isolate them or to separate them with an effort to form a distinct and separate nation. While, of course, they are racially one, still the Jews of America, England, France and Italy are no different than their fellow countrymen, of their respective countries, and to go back and establish a separate colony I believe would retard rather than expedite the opportunities of the Jews of the East. Would Retard Opportunities of Jews.

"The only action by the United States Government which I favor is that which we have maintained in the past—the firm insistence upholding Jewish rights and liberties all over the world. We have been fairly successful in Turkey in the past and completely so now. The Russian problem is one of the past. I, therefore, do not approve of appropriate resolutions by Congress in favor of the establishment in Palestine of a Jewish National Centre. Would Uphold Jewish Rights in Dispersion. Considers Russian Problem Settled.

"My views, in general, in regard to the effort of the Jewish people to establish a national home in Palestine are: General Views on Zionism.

"(a) That it is a mistake to do so. I heartily approve of establishing Jewish centres for educational, religious and social betterment in every nation, but I feel strongly that it is a mistake to do so in any one centre for the whole world. For Jewish Centers throughout Dispersion.

"(b) The Jewish question is only one of religion. I believe in absolute liberty of worship, therefore the Jew is entitled to the fullest protection all over the world in that respect. I believe that a great deal of good is still to be worked out in this country among the Jews. It often happens in a new country that the youngest generation are inclined to forget all the good in the teachings of the Jewish religion and acquire all that is bad in that of the customs of their adopted country, and even some Jewish Question Religious Only. Reform Leaders Deviate from Teachings.

165

of the advanced or reformed Jewish leaders are inclined
to depart or deviate somewhat from close observance to
the ancient teachings.

**Mind still
Open.**
"I would be delighted to meet you and have the
benefit of your knowledge on this subject, for I am
seeking all the information that I can get in the course
of the further study of this matter. My mind is still
open on the matter." (Signed) "F. H. LaGuardia."

The American War Congress and Zionism

By Representative George R. Lunn,
Of New York.

"The capture of Palestine and the City of Jerusalem cannot be considered as a tremendous military advantage, but from a political standpoint it is one of the most important events of the present war. It brought a sense of joy to every Jewish heart that is not comparable to any ordinary motion. I sometimes think that the feeling stirred in my own heart when I read the news of the capture of Jerusalem, could not have been more thrilling had I been a member of the Jewish race. *(margin: Jerusalem Capture Political Event.)*

"The Jewish people have always stood in my mind as the givers to the world of ideas and ideals without which life itself would not be worth the living. The teaching of Israel's prophets and the working of her philosophers has done more to advance the world than any military victory, however great. Back of all worthy military endeavors are fundamental ideas, without which a military endeavor is eventually unavailing. Take from the world's treasure house of thought every contribution made by the Jewish race, and the world would be bankrupt. This is not an exaggerated expression, but an expression made after years of appreciation of what has been done for the world by the Jewish people. *(margin: World Would be Bankrupt Without Jewish Contributions.)*

"To my mind, this contribution of high and potent thinking has been based on fundamental philosophy. Ideals demand a setting in the material. Where the material setting is wanting, the ideals continue their effective and aggressive work by means of a conviction that ultimately the ideal will be actualized. During the past centuries the Jewish people have dreamed of a Jewish State, a national home, in the land of their fathers. They have looked forward to the time when the restoration of the Holy Land, and the Holy City to the Jewish people might be an accomplished fact. Amidst bitterest persecutions they still remain loyal to their ideal. Persecution, injustice, multiplied wrongs, never were able to quell within the Jewish heart the longings for and aspirations toward a national home. Much of this persecution has been done by those who accepted as their Great *(margin: Those Who Refuse Justice to the Jew Deny Christianity.)*

167

Teacher, a son of the Jewish race. Wherever Christians have practised injustice toward the Jew, they have gone contrary to the spirit and philosophy of their Great Teacher.

Zionist Realization to Eliminate anti-Semitism.

"To my mind, now has come the day when, by the restoration of the Holy Land to the Jewish people and the establishment of a national home, the old bitterness may be forever forgotten.

Let America Support Declaration.

"The British Government favors the establishment in Palestine of a national home for the Jewish people, and has pledged itself to facilitate the achievement of this object. It is most fitting, therefore, that our own country, the exponent of democracy, should give its fullest measure of support to the successful prosecution of this historic undertaking in behalf of justice and liberation.

Rapprochement of Occident and Orient.

"The Jewish people in largest numbers have become settled in the occident, but they are essentially connected in thought and history to the orient. Is it not possible that the establishment of a national home for the Jewish people in Palestine might create a State where the Jewish people, free to express their own high and inspiring ideals, might be the terms of rapprochement between the people of the occident and the people of the orient.

No Gain in Suppressing any Race.

"To my mind, the present war is a great conflict, bloody and terrible, but essential for the liberation of the people. The world can never advance by the suppression of any race. Every race has its great contribution to make to the wisdom of the world. The establishment of a national home for the Jewish people, would be in perfect accord with the philosophy underlying the present war.

America's Duty to Further Jewish Nationalism.

"I hope and believe that the United States, speaking through her Congress, will pass the resolution I have introduced. It is one of those resolutions, though short, nevertheless fundamental and historical. It will register for the first time, the voice of this great nation in behalf of justice and liberty to that great people who have given to the world the highest in religion and the best in philosophy." (Signed) "GEORGE R. LUNN."

By Representative James P. Maher,
Of New York.

"I am in favor of a Jewish Homeland in Palestine, and believe that the United States Government should take an active interest in the matter, as I believe that the Jewish people are entitled to this consideration." *Approves of Declaration.*

(Signed) "JAMES P. MAHER."

By Representative Luther W. Mott,
Of New York.

"The United States should join England, France, and Italy in favoring the establishment of a Jewish state or nation in Palestine. I fully sympathize with the historic Jewish people in their natural desire to have the homeland of their race freed from Turkish control, and I rejoice with them in the recent triumph of the British army which bids fair to give the movement a wonderful impetus. It is a disgrace that the Christian and Jewish people of the world have for so many years allowed their holy places to be under the government of—what the Armenian massacres prove to be—the most uncivilized of the great or semi-great nations of the world. *United States Should Make Declaration.*

"Should the Zionist movement succeed, the world will be the better in that it will have added a self-governed community, under the protection of the great Christian countries, and in that the Jewish race will be bettered and strengthened by having, as a people of the Allied countries have, a homeland of freedom and of opportunity" *A Homeland Will Strengthen Jewish Position.*

(Signed) "LUTHER W. MOTT."

By Representative Edmund Platt,
Of New York.

Palestine Must Not be Restored to Turkey.

"I approve fully the statement of the Secretary of State for Foreign Affairs of Great Britain favoring the establishment of a National Home for the Jewish people in Palestine, and see no reason why the United States should not make a similar declaration. General Allenby's troops have, as I write this, thrilled the world by their exploits in Palestine, and have already freed most of the original territory of the ten tribes of Israel from the domain of the followers of Islam. Whatever final settlements are made at the close of the war this territory should never be given back to the Turks, and I do not believe the sentiment of the people of any of the great self-governing nations allied in the struggle for the preservation of democracy will consent that it shall ever be given back. No more fitting disposition could be made of this territory, looked upon as the Holy Land by so many millions of people, than to restore it under proper safeguards to the nation which gave it its great place in the history of the world.

Jews at Home Elsewhere.

"I do not feel familiar enough with the plans of the Zionists to express my opinion as to just how this should be accomplished, but the people of the Hebrew race and religion have so greatly multiplied since their expatriation, and have become so thoroughly a part of many other great nations, in most of which they have long since overcome most of the long-standing prejudice against them and are valued as enlightened, progressive and useful citizens, that it is not to be expected that any great **Preserve the Pastoral Life.** proportion of them could or would at this time find a home in Palestine. The country is too small and its resources too slender to support them. May I add that I think that Jew and Christian alike would regret to see the ancient country too greatly modernized, and that any plans for the future should include a preservation to some extent at least of the primitive, pastoral simple life, which has to a considerable degree been preserved there throughout the centuries."

(Signed)   "Edmund Platt."

By Representative Daniel J. Riordan,
Of New York.

"I favor the British declaration for the re-establishment of the Jewish Homeland in Palestine, and suggest appropriate action by the democratic governments to effect the practical consummation of the above declaration." (Signed)   "D. J. RIORDAN."

Practical Consummation of Declaration.

By Representative Frederick W. Rowe,
Of New York.

"I am very glad that the English Army has taken Jerusalem and a large part of Judea. I do not believe that any great number of the Jewish people of America will ever want to return to Jerusalem for a permanent residence, but I do believe that Jerusalem and the surrounding territory should be either a separate nation or under the government of one of the civilized nations of the world and not be placed again under Mohammedan rule."   (Signed)   "FREDERICK W. ROWE."

An Autonomous Government for Palestine.

By Representative Isaac Siegel,
Of New York.

"I approve of the declarations of England, France and Italy.

"With the successful termination of the war in which we are engaged I am confident that the dream of the people of the Jewish faith will become a reality."

(Signed)   "ISAAC SIEGEL."

Approves Declaration.

Confident of Success.

171

By Representative Charles Bennett Smith, Of New York.

Jewish Centre Desirable.

"It is my belief that the American Government should join the British, French and Italian Governments with respect to the establishment of a National Home for the Jewish people of Palestine. The reasons for such a home appear so obvious that they do not require elaboration. The reasons, however, includes the desirability for a Jewish centre. Social, sentiment, intellectual and historical advantage would inure from the establishment of the proposed home. I feel sure every Jewish and Christian student of race or religion or human progress will see the noble purpose of the movement to carry out the ambitious but thoroughly practicable enterprise."

(Signed) "CHARLES BENNETT SMITH."

By Representative Thomas F. Smith, Of New York.

Supports Declaration.

"The Balfour declaration in favor of the establishment in Palestine of a national home for the Jewish people, which has been indorsed by the French and Italian governments, has my unqualified support.

"I believe in the principles of Zionism, as laid down by the late Theodore Herzl, in order that the Jews, now dispersed over the face of the earth, may return to their homeland, and again set themselves up as a nation.

Favors Resolution. Pledges Support.

"I heartily indorse the contents of President Wilson's letter of August 31st to the Zionist Organization. I construe this as 'favorable action by the United States Government' (with President Wilson as our spokesman), and as indorsement of the Balfour declaration. I would be glad to lend my support to such a resolution.

"As to my general views in regard to the efforts of the Jewish people to establish a national home in Palestine, I might add that from my personal knowledge of the Jews of America, their support of the Zionist movement will in no way affect their whole-hearted Americanism, their allegiance or their loyalty.

End of Long Exile.

"In conclusion, let me congratulate you upon the success which your movement has met, with the hope that the peace which is now beginning to be seen in the rifting clouds, will soon mark the end of the homelessness of the Jewish people." (Signed) "THOMAS F. SMITH."

By Representative Homer P. Snyder,
Of New York.

"I note the project of establishing a Jewish Homeland in Palestine and beg to say that at the proper time and under proper conditions and with the assent of the allied governments, it seems to me there could be no possible exception to this move. The history of the Hebrew people is linked with Palestine, and their help in any movement which will tend to visualize and mark that sentiment would, in my opinion, be most appropriate."

Strengthen Bond with Palestine.

(Signed) "H. P. Snyder."

By Representative Christopher D. Sullivan,
Of New York.

"I heartily approve of the British declaration for a publicly, legally secured home for the Jews in Palestine and trust that our country will unite with the Allies in demanding, as the victors of the great war, that all nationalities, large or small, be restored to their own historic lands.

Fruits of Victory.

"It is my firm belief that the realization of the aims of Zionism is the most practical solution of the eternal Jewish Question, and I shall do all I can to hasten its realization, to the end that the Jew will at last cease to journey as a wanderer and take his place in his ancient home, which is destined to become a nation among nations.

Solution of Jewish Question.

"I favor action by Government and by Congress."

For United States Action.

(Signed) "Christopher D. Sullivan."

By Representative Oscar William Swift,
Of New York.

Democracies
Must
Indorse
Zionism.

"The declaration made by the Honorable Arthur J. Balfour, Secretary of State for Foreign Affairs, on November 2, 1917, in behalf of the British Government, favoring the establishment in Palestine of a National Home for the Jewish people, and which declaration received the official endorsement of the French and Italian governments on February 11, 1918, and February 23, 1918, respectively, should, in my opinion, receive similar endorsement by all nations espousing the cause of Liberty, Civilization and Humanity, and I should, indeed, be pleased to see our great and glorious Government place itself on record accordingly, thereby following out its traditions of the 'Spirit of '76.'

Pledges
Support.

"Be assured of my hearty co-operation to promote the success of your very laudable object which I sincerely hope will also receive the approval of the American Congress by appropriate resolution."

(Signed) "OSCAR WM. SWIFT."

By Representative William F. Waldow,
Of New York.

An Inherent
Right.

"I approve the official declaration of England, France, and Italy on the Zionist question, as I believe that the smaller nations of the world should have a homeland of their own.

A Condition
of Peace.

"I favor the action of the United States Government in conformity with the British declaration at the time when negotiations for peace will be held, as the action to be taken is one for the President, Senate, and State Department. I do not believe that the House can very well act at the present time.

Merits
Approval
of All.

"The efforts being made to establish a national home should receive the hearty approval of all."

(Signed) "WM. F. WALDOW."

By Representative Charles B. Ward,
Of New York.

"I am heartily in favor of the Zionist movement, primarily so on account of the President's declaration of August 31. I think that the bringing about of the re-establishment of the Jewish nation in Palestine should depend to a great extent upon the wishes of the Jewish people themselves." (Signed) "CHARLES B. WARD."

Re-establishment Depends on Jews.

By Representative Hannibal L. Godwin,
Of North Carolina.

"I am unqualifiedly for the British Declaration and Zionist movement and will warmly support a resolution to that effect when it comes up for consideration."

(Signed) "H. L. GODWIN."

Will Support Resolution.

By Representative John H. Small,
Of North Carolina.

"I endorse the declarations of England, France and Italy, and primarily because it will fulfill a long cherished aspiration and will afford the Jews of every nationality the satisfaction of realizing that their race possesses a national centre from which in good time will radiate ideals and movements for the benefit of the Jewish people. I also favor action by the Government of the United States at some appropriate time in the future, and I think a contemporaneous declaration by Congress along the same line would be eminently appropriate and desirable." (Signed) "JNO. H. SMALL."

National Centre.

For Action by Congress and Executive.

By Representative Charles W. Stedman,
Of North Carolina.

Will Support
Jewish
Position.

"I cordially endorse the Zionist movement if such be the wish of the Jewish people.

No Race
Has Con-
tributed
More.

"Amongst our own people the Jew has ever been a conservative force. He has never attempted to disturb existing conditions. His influence has been healthful and his life has been distinguished for charity, benevolence, and philanthropy. His record compares well with any other class anywhere. The history of no race of men, from the early dawn of time, is so full of wonderful events; is so connected with the advance of civilization; is so gilded with strange romance; is so blessed with heroic memories; is more closely allied with the highest truths of science. No race has contributed more to the civilization, prosperity and happiness of humanity, or has survived so much suffering without a surrender of manhood.

"Persecution and oppression have ennobled the character of this people, and they have been led thereby toward greater efforts for moral and intellectual growth. Suffering is necessary to purify both individuals and nations. No man or woman ever reached the high degree of excellence to which their nature might aspire unless exalted by sacrificial fire and these people more than any other in the world's history have exemplified this great truth.

"Centuries have witnessed their struggle. In spite of dispersion and oppression, which robbed them of the simplest rights of man, the development of their intellectual life has been continuous and has preserved for other nations the foundation and basis of morality. They have furnished names renowned as philosophers, musicians, sculptors, and scientific physicians.

"They have preserved a community of faith and ideals founded on an intellectual and moral life which has ever distinguished them and has made them an example for the civilized world. If there be heroism in endurance, in patient fulfillment of duty, in earnest endeavor for good, then Jews have lived heroic lives.

176

"I shall vote with great pleasure for any resolution in Congress in accordance with the declarations heretofore made by England, France, Italy, and our own country, chiefly for the reason that it would be recognition of the Jewish race as a distinct nationality to which they are entitled as fully as any people on the globe."

Will Support Resolution. Recognizes Nationality.

(Signed)   "CHAS. W. STEDMAN."

By Representative Zebulon Weaver,
Of North Carolina.

Endorses Declaration. "None of the victories of the Allied arms brought more genuine happiness than those in Mesopotamia and the expulsion of the Turk from Jerusalem and Palestine. I am in accord with the British Declaration proposing the establishment of a national home for the Jews in the land of their fathers. I do not understand that it is contemplated that the Jews in America shall abandon their allegiance to this Republic, but that in a broad sense the Holy Land is again to pass under the control of the Race that gave to the world the glories of Hebrew traditions and the blessings of a religion that has conquered wherever it has been taught.

Jews everywhere Preserved Racial Integrity. "Senator Zebulon B. Vance, one of the Governors and Senators from my own commonwealth—the State of North Carolina—prepared and delivered a lecture upon "The Scattered Nation." He was a great admirer of the Jewish race. In this address he compared this race to the Gulf Stream which has its origin in the warm and life-giving waters of the Gulf of Mexico and flows northward, through the Atlantic, toward the Arctic. Like a great river flowing through the cold and inhospitable waters of the Atlantic, never losing itself nor its characteristics, it brings warmth and comfort to otherwise desolate shores. So, he said, has been the Jewish Race. It has flowed through all lands and lived under all Governments, but has never been dissipated nor lost, throughout its centuries of wandering.

Turkish Domination a Blot. "This race has contributed in a large and liberal measure to our literature and law. From it has come great statesmen, financiers and soldiers; and above all, from it the world has received its knowledge and conception of the one true and living God. The nations of the earth have been and will continue to be ruled from Sinai. That these holy places have been in the hands of the Turks for so many centuries, has been a blot upon the nations who believe in our one God.

Restore Holy Land to Jews. "Now, that they are rescued through the glorious triumph of the Allied and American arms, they should be returned to the control of the descendants of their ancient masters. I trust that our nation will take proper action to this end." (Signed) "ZEBULON WEAVER."

By Representative J. M. Baer,
Of North Dakota.

"The armies of the Allies have driven from the Holy
Land the followers of the false prophet. They have freed
Israel from its bondage and set up again the hope that
never dies either in the heart of the Jew or Christian;
that some day the children of Judah will once more
possess the land of their fathers. It has been a long
night and the day star has been slow in dawning—but
day begins to break over the world and over Palestine.
Jewish regiments are helping to rescue the land of their
fathers and they with the Gentiles of the West, British
and French, are sweeping the filthiness of the Moslem
and the Turk out of God's Holy Places on earth. This
is the news of the day. It is an earnest of what we
shall bring to other lands. To Belgium, to Serbia, to
Roumania, to Bohemia, to all the oppressed. It has been
a horrible war—a seemingly causeless and useless war.
But no event is useless or causeless in God's providence.
His eternal decrees unroll, in the fullness of time, and
the great plan as it unfolds itself out of the womb of
time becomes clear to human understanding.

"As a Nation we shuddered to take the awful plunge
into this war. As a people we cried out against the loss
of blood and treasure we knew it meant for us. We
cried out that God should suffer such an evil to befall us.
We needed but a little faith to take hold of Him and to
trust Him, that the eternal purpose toward mankind is
but good. Not only the redemption of Israel is brought
near—the redemption of the entire world approaches.
The establishment of a Jewish state in Palestine meets
with my hearty approval. The race that has contributed
to the world so much in art, commerce, and constructive
genius, is about to realize its age-long dream. The
movement appeals to the imagination of the Gentiles of
all lands as well as to the descendants of Israel. The
success of this splendid experiment will mean a secure
and lasting peace for all mankind."

(Signed) "J. M. Baer."

Jews Fight for Palestine.

Approves of Jewish State.

By Representative George M. Young,
Of North Dakota.

Indorses
Establish-
ment of
Homeland.

"I wish to express my entire sympathy with the establishment of a Jewish homeland in Palestine in accordance with the official declarations of England, France and Italy."

(Signed)   "GEORGE M. YOUNG."

By Representative Clement Brumbaugh,
Of Ohio.

Liberals
Must
Rejoice.

"Every student of the Scriptures, every student of History, as well as every lover of Liberty and Justice, will rejoice to see a successful conclusion of your effort to establish a Jewish homeland in Palestine. What a world-wide, epoch-making effort that would be.

"I wish you most abundant success."

(Signed)   "CLEMENT BRUMBAUGH."

By Representative Horatio C. Claypool,
Of Ohio.

Approves
Declaration.

"I approve the official Declarations of England, France, and Italy, on the Zionist question.

Action by
Government
and Con-
gress.

"I favor action by the United States Government in line with the British Declaration. I also favor the adoption of an appropriate resolution by Congress in favor of the establishment in Palestine of a Jewish National Centre.

Entitled to
Palestine.

"If the Jews want a home in Palestine they are entitled to it, it having been their home thousands of years ago."

(Signed)   "H. C. CLAYPOOL."

**By Representative Robert Crosser,
Of Ohio.**

"I approve of the declaration of the British Government on the subject in question. I consider it not only just but highly desirable that the Jewish people should have the opportunity of living under a government which would reflect the views of their race, and so enable them to express more fully the Jewish character. In a general way, it seems to me that this is the right of every race, when it is possible and consistent with the rights of other peoples. The ideals of any race can best be carried out under a government administered in accordance with the views of that race. I favor action by the United States Government in accordance not only with the British declaration, but with the views which I have herein expressed. *(margin: Provides Opportunity for Self-Expression.)*

"I favor the adoption of an appropriate resolution by Congress in favor of the establishment in Palestine of a Jewish National Center, although I would prefer something more definite and substantial in the way of governmental control than the term 'Jewish Center' would seem to contemplate. *(margin: Would Let Congress Indorse Movement.)*

"As I have already said, I regard it as highly desirable that each race should have an opportunity to express and to carry out its ideals under government administered, so far as is practicable, by the representatives of the race itself." *(margin: Self-Government.)*

(Signed) "Robert Crosser."

**By Representative Henry I. Emerson,
Of Ohio.**

"I assure you that I am in favor of the British Declaration and shall assist all I can to establish the Jewish nation in Palestine. *(margin: Will Assist Re-establishment.)*

"I feel Congress should assist and this country should act in conjunction with the other countries of Europe in re-establishing all the smaller nations of the world. *(margin: Wishes Government and Congress Action.)*

"However, we welcome to this country all the Jewish people who desire to come here and live, and make this country their home. The Jew makes a good citizen and a loyal and patriotic American." *(margin: Jews also Welcome Here.)*

(Signed) "H. I. Emerson."

By Representative Simeon D. Fess,
Of Ohio.

Biblical Prophecy Realized by Democracies.

"The desire and movement for the re-establishment of the Jewish nation in their historic land is not only a sentiment age-long that ought to be realized, but an ancient prophecy to be fulfilled through the aid of the western world. It is a welcome and glad situation, brought about by this terrible war, that this biblical prophecy should come to realization through the aid of the democracies of the world, in which this country plays its part so prominently.

England Deserves Congratulations.

"The Jews will not be the only people whose national salvation will become a reality after this war. They will, however, be perhaps the oldest people in that group, whose hopes and aspirations for their return to the Holy Land has won the admiration of the entire civilized world. The Government of Great Britain surely deserves high recognition and hearty congratulations at being the first in our allied group to initiate the movement to satisfy the aspirations of Zionism, as shown in its official Declaration by its Secretary of State for Foreign Affairs, the Honorable Arthur J. Balfour.

Will Vote for Resolution.

"I do not hesitate to say that I shall be very glad to vote for a resolution, expressing the principles laid down in the British Declaration specifically, and in the Zionist ideals generally, whenever such resolution would be proposed in Congress.

Pledges Help.

"I am very glad of the opportunity to make these sentiments known, and will, as in the past, do my utmost to help the Jewish people, or nation, in every possible way."

(Signed)   "SIMEON D. FESS."

By Representative Warren Gard,
Of Ohio.

"The continuance of a people in maintaining racial strength of character and the desire of such people for a National Home are seemingly to me the high substance of the official Declarations of England, France and Italy.

Preservation of Race.

"The re-occupation of the ancient territory will be alike sentimental and practical, affording instance of permanent control by influences potential for good and the possible territorial development of a nation. This is eminently a matter for the Jewish people themselves and to be worked out by them.

Reoccupation Sentimental and Practical.

"That there be no abridgment of the rights of political status of the Jews in any country or indeed of any people in any country, and that all peoples recognizing and obeying the law be afforded its full protection, is the goal of national and international achievement today."

No Abridgment of Rights.

(Signed)   "WARREN GARD."

By Representative William Gordon,
Of Ohio.

"I personally favor the Zionist movement, and assure you that it has my hearty sympathy, because I believe it would be of material, spiritual, and cultural aid not only to the Jews who may return or desire to return to the land of their ancestors but would be of real sentimental value to the Jews all over the world.

Favors Movement— Benefits All Jews.

"I feel that this ambition on the part of the Jews is a very laudable and praiseworthy one and that it will eventually win the support and co-operation of the civilized world, thereby atoning in part for the injustice done to the Jewish people in many lands for thousands of years."

Will Win World Support.

(Signed)   "WILLIAM GORDON."

By Representative David A. Hollingsworth,
Of Ohio.

Heartily
Indorses
Project.

"I now take time simply to say that I heartily endorse the suggestions for the establishment of a Jewish Homeland in Palestine."

(Signed)   "D. A. HOLLINGSWORTH."

By Representative Roscoe C. McCulloch,
Of Ohio.

Approves
Declarations.

"I take pleasure in saying that I entirely approve and am in sympathy with the Declarations of our Allies in favor of a Jewish homeland in Palestine."

(Signed)   "ROSCOE C. McCULLOCH."

By Representative Isaac R. Sherwood,
Of Ohio.

Favors
Resolution
and Government Action.

"I will say my sympathies are entirely in accord with the official declarations by England, France and Italy on the Zionist question. I am now, and always have been, in favor of the largest liberties to all peoples and the absolute protection of these rights, which should be regarded as sacred.

"I favor action by the United States Government in alliance with the above declaration, and I strongly favor the adoption of an appropriate resolution in Congress, and will vote for such resolution, if given the opportunity. My views on all these questions are well known to my Jewish friends in Toledo, where I reside.

"I likewise favor a National Home in Palestine for the Jewish people, and am in favor, absolutely, of giving the right of determining their own future to all peoples and all nationalities, as well as a right to worship God in accordance to the dictates of their own conscience."   (Signed)   "ISAAC R. SHERWOOD."

By Representative John S. Snook,
Of Ohio.

"I wish to take the opportunity to express my entire Pledges
sympathy with your movement to establish a National Support.
Home for the Jewish people in Palestine. Tradition and
sentiment appeal to me as strong reasons why this
should be done but I also believe it would result in very
great practical good to your race.

"I will be glad to lend the movement my hearty
support."   (Signed)   "JOHN S. SNOOK."

By Representative Benjamin F. Welty,
Of Ohio.

"I am gratified with the movement to establish a Gratified
home for the Jews in Palestine."   With
                                                Movement.
(Signed)   "B. F. WELTY."

By Representative Charles D. Carter,
Of Oklahoma.

"The British Declaration favoring the establishment For
in Palestine of a National Home for the Jewish people Independent
is somewhat indefinite, and the word 'home' is so gen- Jewish
eral in its application, that I am at a loss to understand State.
the full meaning of a National Home for the Jewish
people in Palestine. If it means that the Jews are at
last to be given an opportunity to establish a Government of their own in a country of their own, then I
know of no reason why any man in this country should
oppose any such worthy proposition.

"In America, as in all other countries where they Indications
have settled, the Jewish people have given evidence of of Success.
the very highest type of virility and intellectuality. I
have no doubt that a country governed in accordance
with Jewish ideas would soon aspire to be one of the
powers of the world."
(Signed)   "C. D. CARTER."

185

By Representative Tom D. McKeown,
Of Oklahoma.

Approves Declarations.

"I am absolutely in accord with the Zionist movement; not only this, but I am heartily in sympathy with this movement and with the Declarations of Great Britain, France, and Italy, which will cause this movement to become a fact and a reality.

Palestine Logical Home.

"I have studied this question for a long while, have followed up the development of the idea since the first day when the Rothschilds started colonization in Palestine. I have watched the various plans of the territorialists but I have always felt that the historic and logical place for a Jewish state is their ancient and beloved home, Palestine.

Jewish State Source of Inspiration.

"It is a happy coincidence that along with the realization and aspirations of the great democratic idealists of the world will also come the realization of the dream of ages, that has absorbed the Jewish people in their history. I am inclined to feel in this matter along these lines because of my natural sympathies for a people that for thousands of years have been wandering all over the world without any country which they may, as a unit or as a group, call their own; because my heart always went out to a people who spoke every tongue except their own. I have long felt that the time has come that this unfair treatment and discrimination against the Jews all over the world come to a halt, and that a new nation, the re-birth of the oldest nation in history, be again formed to the delight of its own sons and daughters as well as to the inspiration of the entire Christian world.

Accords with Wilson's Principles.

"I certainly do not hesitate to state that the Jewish people are easily to be included as one of the group of small nationalities who are to decide their own fate, in accordance with the principles laid down by our great President, Woodrow Wilson. The small nationalities, the Jews and the others, should have the right to live and exist in accordance with their national aspirations and hopes and to share the things put here by the great world Creator.

"I am in favor of a resolution to be introduced into Congress purporting the re-establishment of the Jewish nation in Palestine, conditioned upon the fact that such resolution come up at the time when it would cause no embarrassment to us or our Allies and when it would not be thought to be anti-diplomatic, from the standpoint of the great democracies of the world." Favors
Congress
Resolution.

(Signed) "TOM D. McKEOWN."

By Representative Dick T. Morgan,
Of Oklahoma.

"I personally sympathize with the aspiration of the Jews, and would be glad to give my encouragement to the Zionist movement. Favors
Zionist
Movement.

"I have read the statements made by the representatives of England, France, and Italy, relative thereto, and I see no reason why the said statements would not receive the hearty approval of the people of the United States. Merits
Approval of
American
People.

"I think that you and other leaders of the Jews of the United States are engaged in a movement which deserves the sympathy, encouragement, and support of all broad-minded men throughout the world." Deserves
World
Support.

(Signed) "DICK T. MORGAN."

By Representative Willis C. Hawley,
Of Oregon.

Re-establish-ment Act of Justice.

"The declarations of the officials of England, France, and Italy, in favor of establishing a National Home for the Jewish people in the land their race has forever made famous is one of the fortunate results of the war. These great and humane nations have seen their neighbors driven out by a barbarous invader and rendered suddenly and unexpectedly homeless. Their sympathies so violently appealed to by the misfortunes of war, have extended to a race which has been without a national home for eighteen hundred years.

Wants Homeland under Allied Protection.

"Through the people of Israel there were given laws and teachings which have proven the enduring foundations of religion, orderly government, liberty, obedience, devotion to duty, and love of country. Every nation that has heeded these laws and teachings has prospered. One of the bravest fights for liberty ever made was that of the Jews under the Maccabees. I am in favor of giving to them again their homeland, under the protection of the Allied Nations, and a guarantee of the rights and privileges of all people who may live there.

Indorsement in Line with American Policy.

"If my memory of history is not at fault, the United States was the first modern nation to give to the Jews equal rights and privileges with other peoples. It would accord with this policy for the United States to join her allies in this movement, and whatever action may be necessary and proper for us to take, I favor.

God-speed.

"Many nations important in their day have disappeared, the governments they organized disintegrated and the people lost their racial identity. Their work was done. But the Jew is the exception. Through the centuries of persecution and adversity the Jews maintained their racial identity and distinguishing institutions. Turkish misrule has devastated and saddened their once prosperous and populous land. If the Jews wish to rebuild its fortunes, God speed them."

(Signed)   "WILLIS C. HAWLEY."

188

By Representative Earl H. Beshlin,
Of Pennsylvania.

"I approve the Declarations of England, France, and Italy, on the Zionist question, and I can see no reason why our government cannot with propriety adopt a similar resolution. I believe in the eventual fulfillment of prophesy, and this to my mind means the restoration of Palestine to the Jews who by their loyalty to our government are entitled to the support of all patriotic Americans in their efforts to establish a national home in Palestine." *Entitled to American Support.*

(Signed)   "E. H. BESHLIN."

By Representative Guy E. Campbell,
Of Pennsylvania.

"I see no reason why I cannot endorse the movement to establish a Jewish Homeland in Palestine. Certainly these oppressed people are entitled to this recognition. The history of the Christian world began in Palestine, and I believe all Christians everywhere will favor this project in the interest of a race which has contributed so much to the development of ancient and modern civilization." *Indorses Zionism.*

(Signed)   "GUY E. CAMPBELL."

By Representative Henry A. Clark,
Of Pennsylvania.

"If the aspirations of the Jewish people are for the recreation of a national home, if they desire to establish an independent republic of their own, it seems to me that the problem is one that must be largely solved by the genius of the Jewish race. *Favors if Jews Desire It.*

"In reflecting over this subject many things occur to me, but I will not now attempt to discuss them. I have become, however, greatly interested in this matter and propose to give it a more studious consideration." *Become Greatly Interested.*

(Signed)   "HENRY A. CLARK."

189

By Representative Peter E. Costello,
Of Pennsylvania.

Jews may further Contribute to Civilization.

"The Balfour Declaration has for its object the establishment of a National Home for the Jewish people in order that those may return to Palestine, who, by reason of persecution in foreign lands, have been unable to develop along normal lines. A home would be provided, also, for those who prefer to live a specifically Jewish life in order that the Jewish people might make further contributions to civilization.

True Aim of Zionism.

"It is not the aim of Zionism, as I understand it, to influence all of the Jewish people to return to the Holy Land, because a majority of those now living under free institutions are contented and happy, and are powerful factors in fostering and developing the spirit of Democracy and Freedom.

British Declaration.

"Again, it is officially set forth by the British Declaration which promises that 'nothing shall be done which may prejudice the rights and political status enjoyed by Jews in other countries.' I believe the establishment of a Homeland in Palestine for the Jewish people will materially aid, also, those who prefer to live in other countries.

Affords Opportunity for Normal Development.

"I am happy that the Allies have declared in favor of a movement which has so much of spiritual and moral value. The Hebrew race has in many centuries made the most valuable contributions in all fields of human endeavor. If allowed to develop in a normal way in its own State, and under its own institutions, there is every reason to believe that it will in the future make further contributions and materially add to the cultural values of the world. It is difficult to understand how anyone familiar with the history of the Jewish people can interpose any objection to an effort to right the wrongs of centuries—a movement founded upon the dictates of Natural Justice." (Signed) "PETER E. COSTELLO."

By Representative Thomas S. Crago,
Of Pennsylvania.

"I heartily approve of the declarations of England, France and Italy on the Zionist question. I believe that the desire of the Jewish people themselves should be followed in any movement looking to the establishment of a national home in Palestine. Many of the Jewish people are so articulated with the social and industrial activities of our country that this matter perhaps does not appeal to them as strongly as to the members of this race who have given the matter personal study and consideration. *Approves Declaration of Allies.*

"I would be in favor of action by the United States Government along the line of the British declaration, and can see no reason why this action cannot well be taken at the present moment. Many of the Jewish people are now giving their lives on the field of battle that our national ideals may prevail in this great conflict; and by their patriotism to this country they have demonstrated the fact that citizenship here means much to them. The idealism and pride of ancestry which leads members of the Jewish race to long for a recognition and a place in the home of their ancestors is to be commended. *Commends Jewish National Aspirations.*

"I shall be very glad, indeed, to keep in touch with this work and assist the movement in any way I can."

(Signed) "THOMAS S. CRAGO."

By Representative George P. Darrow,
Of Pennsylvania.

"I am heartily in accord with the movement to establish a Jewish Homeland in Palestine in accordance with the official declarations of our Allies. I fully recognize the many fine qualities of the Jewish people, and if, as I understood, it is their ambition and desire to establish such a community, I shall be glad to render any possible assistance to them, either in supporting an appropriate resolution by Congress or otherwise." *Will Support Congress Resolution.*

(Signed) "GEORGE P. DARROW."

By Representative George W. Edmonds,
Of Pennsylvania.

Approves
Declaration.
"I heartily approve of the action of England, France and Italy on the Zionist question.

Sees Justice
of Claims.
"For centuries the Jewish people have been without a national existence, and have been scattered among all the nations of the earth. They have, however, been able to produce many of the leaders of thought and action in all lines of endeavors, and it would seem only proper that they should have a home country where they can have a distinct nationality, showing the world their capabilities.

Wants Our
Government
to Act.
"I would be in favor of action on the part of the United States Government along similar lines of that of the English Government, and believe that it should be done at as early a date as possible."

(Signed)   "G. W. EDMONDS."

The American War Congress and Zionism

By Representative John R. Farr,
Of Pennsylvania.

"It was very gratifying to me to learn of the declarations in favor of a Jewish Homeland in Palestine, as issued by the governments of Great Britain, France and Italy. I was particularly delighted to read that great letter in support of Zionism, written by President Wilson to the Zionists of America. I am thoroughly in sympathy with this fine movement for the restoration of the Jews to their old home, a restoration which has come to the children of Jacob after waiting for it impatiently for many centuries. *Thoroughly Sympathizes with Movement.*

"Let it be clearly understood, as the Balfour declaration well states it, that not only will the civil and religious rights of the non-Jewish communities in Palestine not suffer in the least by this newly established Jewish State in that land, but also that all the Jews in the many other lands shall not be deprived of any political and social rights. *Rights for Inhabitants.*

"As I understand it, there are about fourteen million Jews in the world. Palestine at present can accommodate but one-fifth of that number. It is possible that later on Greater Palestine may be able to accommodate comfortably about one-third of the Jews of the world. Thus it must be very evident that the great majority of the Jews will still remain in the countries where they are now. I do not believe that the Jews in the more enlightened countries will go to Palestine to any great extent. In fact, that is not necessary nor even desirable or possibly wanted by the Zionists themselves. If the new Jewish State will become the real genuine home for that minority of the Hebrews it will have accomplished its purpose superbly. But I know that it is bound to be more. It will have a tremendous influence on the Jews all over the world in every possible way. It will enhance their old and great civilization, and will bring to them that pride and glory which they had been wanting for two thousand years. *State to Reflect Glory on All Jews.*

"President Wilson has spoken in its favor in words unmistakable. I believe that the country should also *Favors Resolution in Congress.*

193

speak its mind for Zionism and the restoration of these millions of Jews to Palestine through a proper resolution in Congress. I feel certain it will receive the support of everyone, and will be gladly hailed by all Americans."

(Signed) "JOHN R. FARR."

By Representative Benjamin K. Focht,
Of Pennsylvania.

Jewish
Government
for Pales-
tine.

"If it is the hope and ambition of the Jews to have Palestine set apart for a Jewish Government, organized and administered under the consent of the governed, I am heartily in accord with such purpose. In the presence of the world conflict and the hope we all entertain for humanity as an outcome of our successful war against Germany, I should like to see hereafter all governments that are set up founded on the same broad, popular idea which underlies our own great Republic. In other words, the hour has struck for the divine right business to disappear, together with the boiler-plate nobility and the privilege which has gone with these counterfeit masqueraders."

(Signed) "B. K. FOCHT."

By Representative Manlon M. Garland,
Of Pennsylvania.

Favors a
Resolution
by Congress.

"I wish to assure you that I am in entire accord with the project to establish a National Home for the Jewish people in Palestine, and such lawful legislation as may be introduced for that purpose I shall gladly support while in Congress."

(Signed) "M. M. GARLAND."

By Representative George Scott Graham,
Of Pennsylvania.

"I have read with interest the declaration of the *Approves Declaration.* Honorable Arthur J. Balfour, and I approve and am entirely in accord with the sentiment expressed therein.

"I am of the opinion that the establishment of a *Restoration entirely Fitting.* National Homeland in Palestine would be in accordance with the eternal fitness of things. There is no land in the world toward which the thoughts of all Christian people turn with greater intensity of interest than to the land of Palestine.

"The restoration of a national life for the Jewish *Will Improve Jewish Status.* people would help to give them a greater place and standing in the world. They have survived misfortunes, persecutions and oppressions, and made for themselves notwithstanding all these detracting and depressing influences, an enviable place among the people wherein they dwell.

"I would favor action of the United States Government in line with the British declaration not at the present moment but in the future, and an expression in the *Favors Congressional Legislation.* form of a resolution by Congress favoring the establishment in Palestine of the Jewish National Centre."

(Signed) "GEORGE S. GRAHAM."

By Representative M. Clyde Kelly,
Of Pennsylvania.

"Permit me to congratulate you on the splendid *Conquerors never Assimilated Zion.* work you are doing for the establishment of a Jewish Homeland in Palestine. The dream of devoted men and women for centuries is soon to become an established fact. History records the fact that no invading nation has ever really conquered Zion. Successive waves of assailants rolled over Palestine but none of them assimilated it. The Turks have only been barbarian possessors, ruling as outsiders. Always, the sons of Abraham remained undestroyed as a distinct and noble race, awaiting the day of homecoming. That day is almost here and all who are hastening its coming are to be commended, whoever they are and wherever they are."

(Signed) "M. CLYDE KELLY."

By Representative Edgar R. Kiess,
Of Pennsylvania.

Favors
Declara-
tions.

"I wish to say that personally I favor the establishment of a Jewish Homeland in Palestine in accordance with the official declarations of the United States, Great Britain, France, and Italy."

(Signed)   "EDGAR R. KIESS."

By Representative Aaron S. Kreider,
Of Pennsylvania.

Approves
Declara-
tions.

"I am glad to have the opportunity to say that I thoroughly approve the official Declarations of England, France, and Italy on the Zionist question.

Common-
Sense View
and For-
ward Step.

"The British Government is to be complimented on the common-sense view and forward step they have taken. The re-establishment of the Jewish Nation in its historic land is a sentiment of long standing, and it is to be hoped that the Western World, and the United States in particular, will lend its influence to this movement.

Favors
Congress
Resolution.

"I shall be very glad to support any appropriate resolution on the part of Congress in favor of the establishment in Palestine of a Jewish Homeland."

(Signed)   "A. S. KREIDER."

By Representative J. Hampton Moore,
Of Pennsylvania.

"The views of the foreign potentiaries as expressed
in the Allied Declarations for a Jewish Homeland in
Palestine, impressed me favorably as tending to bring
about some international understanding that would
vouchsafe the solidity and permanence of the insti-
tution desired.

Favorably Impressed by Declarations.

"It would certainly be helpful if such international encouragement could be secured. I assume, however, that
the nations will take time to inquire into such details
of the plan as might involve the rights of other people
not directly participating in the Zionist scheme. The
Zionists, no doubt, will strive in due course to make
these matters known throughout the world.

Secure the Nations' Co-operation.

"Realizing the difficulties the Jewish people have en-
countered through the centuries and are now encounter-
ing in certain foreign countries to hold and sustain a just
and deserved status in matters civil and political, I
would hope that their ambition to attain what is called
'a Jewish National Center' might ultimately be realized.
There will be reason to rejoice when it can no longer be
said of the Jew that he is a man without a country."

Jewish People Homeless No Longer.

(Signed) "J. Hampton Moore."

By Representative John M. Morin,
Of Pennsylvania.

Entire Sympathy With Declarations.

"I am in entire sympathy with the declaration contained in the letter of Mr. A. J. Balfour, Secretary of State for Foreign Affairs, dated November 2, 1917, and addressed to Lord Rothschild. That letter states that the British Declaration of sympathy with Zionistic aspirations had been submitted and approved by the English Cabinet. Further declarations to the same end have also been put forth by France and Italy.

Indorses Basle Program.

"I am in favor of establishing in Palestine that kind of a home which is contemplated by the organic law of the Zionist movement as formulated in the Basel program of August, 1897. This program was adopted by the first Congress of Jews which met at Basel in Switzerland under the leadership of the great Dr. Theodore Herzl. Its basic declaration was that the object of Zionism is the creation for the Jewish people of a home in Palestine, secured by public international law. This is to say, there can not be established in Palestine any great home for the Jewish people which shall not be approved by civilized public opinion, as embodied in the organic law of the world. These great ideas are given further exposition by the eminent Mr. Justice Louis Brandeis in the following language:

Accepts Expression of Brandeis.

" 'Zionism seeks to establish in Palestine, for such Jews as choose to go and remain there, and for their descendants, a legally secured home, where they may live together and lead a Jewish life, where they may expect ultimately to constitute a majority of the population, and may look forward to what we should call home rule.'

Indorsement Does not Impair Loyalty to America.

"In view of these facts, I can not see how anybody, Jewish or non-Jewish, can be opposed to Zionist aspirations. It seems to me that any Jew who is a Zionist must be not alone a better Jew for that fact, but also a better American, because by supporting the Zionistic ideal he is supporting the liberty of his own great and distinguished race in the world, while at the same time not in the slightest impairing the loyalty which he owes first and above all to America. Intelligent non-Jews

can certainly find nothing in the Zionist platform which
is not in thorough accord with the democratic traditions
of America and the principles of peace as they have been
enunciated by President Wilson.

"It is the hope of America that in Abraham Lincoln's
phrase 'all men everywhere may be free'; and that all
peoples, whether great or small, shall have the right to
work out their own destinies unhampered by tyranny.
The Jewish people have suffered perhaps more than any
other people from persecution of various kinds. It is
only an act of justice that not alone shall full civil and
religious rights be granted to them in all lands, but that
they shall have the right to establish in their ancient
home a land of their own where such pioneering spirits
among them as may desire to do so shall be free to set
up characteristic Jewish institutions and to build up a
characteristic Jewish life and culture.

Free to Establish Jewish Institutions.

"There is no compulsion in the Zionistic movement,
as I understand it, that any man in any land shall return
to Zion. It does not contemplate a removal of all the
Jews of the world to Palestine, because Palestine at most
could not accommodate more than one-fifth of the fourteen million Jews that there are in the world.

No Compulsion in Movement.

"To my mind the establishment of a national home
for the Jewish people seems practicable, when we consider that in twenty years between the Basel program of
August, 1897, and the declaration of the British Government of November, 1917, the Jewish people have established over forty colonies in the Holy Land, have revivi-
fied the Hebrew language, have organized the Zionistic
movement in all civilized lands, and have already given
to the world through this movement such great leaders as
Herzl, Aaronsohn, the discoverer of wild wheat, Weizmann, the head of the English Zionists, and have been
able to arouse the sympathy and labors of such men as
Max Nordau, Sokolow, Lord Rothschild, Justice Brandeis, and innumerable other great men.

Colonization and Hebrew Revival Augur Success.

"There are a number of Jewish people in my con-
stituency, and from my personal contact with them I
know that the Zionistic movement has been a splendidly

Holds Promise for Jews and non-Jews.

idealistic one. Any movement which can bring such fruits of a deeper and better life to a people, and promise correspondingly great contributions to the world, must surely be supported by all men to whom the cause of liberty and of free life for all peoples, no matter how great or how small, is dear.

Executive Action. Congress Resolution.

"Under the circumstances I cannot but favor action by the United States Government in line with the British declaration as soon as that may seem wise to the Executive, for it is on the part of the Executive that such action must be looked forward to under our system of government. I, personally, would be strongly in favor of the adoption of an appropriate resolution by Congress in favor of the establishment in Palestine of a Jewish National center."   (Signed)   "JOHN M. MORIN."

By Representative Edward E. Robbins,
Of Pennsylvania.

Jews Must Work Out Their Destiny.

"I have not given this matter any special thought. My idea of it is that the Jewish people should determine their own destiny, and that no government should interfere or attempt to establish the Jewish people in any part of the world as a segregated people or interfere with their working out their own future. One of the results of this war will be to bring about better understanding among the various nations of the world and among the various religious denominations of the world and I believe much of the prejudice that has existed between these divisions of men will disappear.

No Governmental Intervention in Future.

"We are about to enter upon a period of universal brotherhood of man and fatherhood of God, and government upon a higher plane, religion upon lines laid down in the Old and New Testament by the prophets and by our Lord. I think the future holds for all of us better conditions, nobler opportunities for service for each other, and I believe in this new period of the world, upon which we are about to enter, that the people of the world will work out their own destinies without any government interfering therewith, and among these peoples will be the Jews. Just what that destiny is I am unable to say, but I think they should be permitted to work it out in their own way unhindered and unimpeded."

(Signed)   "EDWARD E. ROBBINS."

200

By Representative John M. Rose,
Of Pennsylvania.

"I am now, and always have been, in accord with the proposition for the establishment in Palestine of a national home for the Jewish people.

Approves of Project.

"My thought is that the declaration of which mention has been made, will only result in bringing about a situation to which the Jewish people of the world are entitled and restore them to conditions which were ruthlessly destroyed without just cause.

Jews Entitled to National Home.

"I have attended a number of meetings of the representative Jewish people in the district I have the honor to represent, and my judgment is that the people in general are in sympathy with the present movement in behalf of the Jew.

"The outstanding feature of the proposition is the fact that no Jew will be compelled to reside within the limits of Palestine should the National Home be established there, and he should rejoice in the fact that his rights are about to be recognized. It remains with him to accept or refuse."   (Signed)   "JOHN M. ROSE."

By Representative Bruce F. Sterling,
Of Pennsylvania.

Jewish
National
Awakening
Inspiring.

"One of the most prominent virtues of any race or nation is its self-consciousness. If a nation or people loses this instinct of self it might just as leave be merged in the strong streams of the rest of humanity and disappear from the earth. It was thought by some that although religiously distinct and self-expressive, the Jews of the world had finally given up their two-score centuries' ambition as a *nation*, and were ready to be absorbed among the other nations of the globe. This, at least, was the conception of the non-Jewish world, and, if I am not mistaken even by some of the children of Israel.

"It is, therefore, most refreshing and inspiring to learn of this great movement of Jewish Nationlism, called Zionism. From the days of Herzl down to the present moment, under the leadership of our own celebrated American citizen, Justice Brandeis, Zionism, as I understand it, has progressed and prospered by leaps and bounds. The former religious aspect of Zionism was augmented, in modern days, by the distinct national spirit of the Jewish leaders of the present. The movement among the Hebrews arouses all the aspiration and hopes and even religious ecstacies, that may have become dormant in these troublesome days, days of revolutions and epoch-making. This is a distinct gain to the combined progress and welfare of the earth as it is to the Jews themselves.

"November 2, 1917, opens a golden page in modern Jewish history. On that day, Great Britain pledged itself in support of Zionism, and for the establishment of a Jewish Homeland in Palestine. This, followed by similar declarations on the part of France and Italy, and all the others who are allied against Germany, brought the Jewish question in its most vital points to the fore in the diplomacy of the world. The solution to this question, with all the democratic powers, including that of the United States, siding with the purposes and aspirations of the Jewish National Movement, will and must be favorable to the Jewish people. I see, as a result of the coming peace, a Jewish nation inhabiting the old Jewish State, prospering in the land of its forefathers, and serving as a guiding post to the religious and ethical movements of all nations."

(Signed) "Bruce F. Sterling."

By Representative Nathan L. Strong,
Of Pennsylvania.

"I have never had occasion to give the matter special study, and my views are based only on the information I have obtained from general reading on the subject. I can, therefore, only state in general terms that I am in sympathy with the movement and approve the several propositions set forth in your communication." *In Sympathy with Zionism.*

(Signed) "Nathan L. Strong."

By Representative Henry W. Temple,
Of Pennsylvania.

"I have read with a great deal of interest the declaration of the British Government favoring the establishment in Palestine of a national home for the Jewish people and the endorsements of this declaration by the French and British Governments. *Wishes Success.*

"I hope the policy thus announced will receive the approval and support of all who may be able to contribute to its accomplishment."

(Signed) "Henry W. Temple."

By Representative Thomas W. Templeton,
Of Pennsylvania.

Wants
Congress
to Act.

"I am in hearty accord with the declarations of England, France, and Italy on the Zionist question, and shall be glad to favor some action on the part of the Congress of the United States expressing our willingness to lend assistance and influence toward making a reality of what the Jewish people have long hoped for, namely, a return to the Holy Land. The Jews are the natural guardians of that land, and the Holy Places therein. Many, of course, would not avail themselves of the opportunity to return because they have become a part of our land and institutions. And it is well that it is so, for we would miss their many sterling qualities manifest in the various activities of our national existence. On the other hand, however, many of the Jewish people would welcome the opportunity to return to the land of their ancestors.

Willing
to Assist.

"I shall be glad to think on this question, and will watch and assist the movement in any way I can."

(Signed) "T. W. TEMPLETON."

By Representative William S. Vare,
Of Pennsylvania.

"I feel that the Jews of the world cannot want to regain their rule over Palestine any more than the Christians want them to regain it. It would take only a small per cent of the Jews of the world to repopulate the Holy Land and re-establish their former home. There are thousands who want to go and there are other thousands who are eager to help them do so should Palestine be restored to the Jews, as outlined in the official British Declaration. These thousands, who are bound to increase into the millions later, will form, with those already there, a nucleus to one of the best future states of the modern world.

"Zionism regained means to the Jews Paradise regained after it had been lost. It will fill the hearts of the Jews in many lands, who are and will remain citizens of those lands, full of joy and pride to know that their ancient land, the land of their civilization and culture, has again been established and a Jewish government formed among the other governments of the world. I would suggest that Jewish representatives, of the future state of Palestine, be requested and invited to attend the deliberations at the peace table, so as to insure absolute justice to them.

"I am in favor of a resolution to be introduced in Congress embodying the ideas I have here expressed and hope that such a step will be taken in the near future."

(Signed) "Wm. S. Vare."

By Representative Henry W. Watson,
Of Pennsylvania.

"I favor the Jewish Homeland in Palestine as declared by England, France and Italy, and will support an appropriate resolution by Congress, if it sets forth the principles as stated in the British declaration."

(Signed) "Henry W. Watson."

Side notes:
To Be Desired by Jews and Gentiles.

For Zionist Representation at Peace Conference.

Hopes Congress Will Act.

Will Support Appropriate Resolution.

By Commissioner Jaime C. DeVeyra,
Of the Philippine Islands.

Indorses
Official
Declara-
tions.

"I am heartily in sympathy with the official declarations of Great Britain, France and Italy, favoring a Jewish Homeland in Palestine, and especially with the enthusiastic statement of President Wilson on the Zionist question. I am anxious to have my voice in favor of the declaration of the British Government, reading as follows:

"His Majesty's Government views with favor the establishment in Palestine of a National Home for the Jewish people and will use its best endeavors to facilitate the achievement of this object, it being clearly understood that nothing shall be done which may prejudice the civil and religious rights of non-Jewish communities in Palestine, or the rights and political status enjoyed by Jews in any other country.

"I will do all I can when the opportunity may present itself to aid it in my own humble way.

For Self-
Determina-
tion with-
out Excep-
tion.

"I am in complete accord with the principles of self-determination of all nationalities as laid down by President Wilson to apply to all peoples and races, certainly with no exception to the Jewish people and to the Jewish nation. Doubtless, you are aware that we, the Philippinos, have been working constantly towards the same end—the freedom and independence of the Philippines, which we hope will be accomplished at a date not far distant. To oppose the aspirations of your people or of any people to establish a free government in their own way would indeed be contrary to our own ideals and principles.

Confident of
Realization.

"I, therefore, sympathize with your cause and feel confident that with the official declarations of the Great Powers above-mentioned, your plan of a future home in Palestine will soon be realized."

(Signed)   "JAIME C. DeVEYRA."

By Commissioner Teodoro R. Yangco,
Of the Philippine Islands.

"I am very much in sympathy with the National aspirations of the Jewish people everywhere for the formation of an independent State in Palestine. I consider an expression of right and justice that England, France and Italy, should have declared themselves in support of this Zionist tendency among the Jews. It is my fond hope and sincere wish that, as a result of this World struggle, the Jewish State may emerge, and I know that it is proper. These expressions on my part are not mere sentiments. They are well founded by reason and understanding of the question and of similar movements. I cannot help but have the greatest trust in Zionism, and have the highest admiration for this Jewish National movement. We Filipinos feel with the Jews in their aspirations, for many of our problems, to a certain degree, are also those of the Jewish problem. The end of the war will mark the independence of the Jewish Nation, which, I hope, would be followed by the independence of the Philippine Islands. I feel that our freedom will be greeted by the Jews of the world just as we Filipinos are ready to greet your rejuvenation. May Zionism prove the solution to the many problems that confronted the Jews for thousands of years."

Philippinos Understand and Appreciate National Hope.

(Signed) "Teodoro R. Yangco."

By Commissioner Felix Cordova Davila,
Of Porto Rico.

Porto Rico
Approves of
Zionists.

"The people of Porto Rico who enjoy the privilege of fighting side by side with their brothers from the States on the farflung battle line in France, are nevertheless by reason of their insular situation, numbered among the "Smaller Peoples" of the Earth, and as such they are in full accord and sympathy with the Zionist Movement.

Appreciates
Self-Government.

"Proud of the honor conferred to us by the great Republic of America we are prompt to contribute to the full measure of our resources in this world war for the establishment of ideals and self-government.

Idea of
National
Center
Appeals.

"That is why the establishment in Palestine of a Jewish National Centre appeals to our people. If the proposed government is organized under guarantees that will not prejudice the civil and religious rights of non-Jewish peoples it must meet with universal approval."

(Signed)   "Felix Cordova Davila."

By Representative George F. O'Shaunessy,
Of Rhode Island.

Wants
Congress
to Act.

"I endorse most heartily the official declaration of Great Britain in favor of the establishment of a National Home in Palestine for the Jewish People, and trust that the American Congress will take similar action in the near future.

Liberals
Indorse
Movement.

"The cherished dreams of the Jewish people would be realized under such action, and their status as a nation established. Every liberal thinker wishes Godspeed to any movement calculated to soften the blows given to the harassed and persecuted Jew, for sugar-coat it as we will he has been persecuted. I wish the movement every success." (Signed)   "G. F. O'Shaunessy."

208

By Representative Walter R. Stiness,
Of Rhode Island.

"I am in favor of the British declaration for a Jewish Homeland in Palestine and would be glad to give this promise my utmost support. I heartily endorse the Zionist movement in the hope that it will solve the Jewish problem forever. I am certain that all liberal-minded people are ready to aid in the achievement of the purposes.

"The end of the war is bound to see a happier world and with this happy world, a spiritual rejoicing of many of the smaller nationalities which have been oppressed by autocratic powers. Perhaps the Jews will more than all others rejoice in this new glory."

Will Assist. Confident of Support of Liberals.

(Signed) "WALTER R. STINESS."

By Representative Samuel J. Nicholls,
Of South Carolina.

"I wish to state that my sympathies are with the Zionists, although I am unable to understand exactly what is meant by 'A National Home.' However, I feel sure that when the statement was issued through the British press on this subject, they meant to use the words in a very broad and far-reaching sense.

Sympathizes with National Hope.

"The Jewish race has had a wonderful career, and has come through in a manner most commendable, and I do not think the rights and religion of this race should be looked at in a prejudiced manner by the civilized world. To my mind I always associate Jerusalem with the Jews and think of no race which has a more sacred right to become the guardians of the city, with its many Holy Associations.

Would See the Jews Guard Jerusalem.

"I hope that the United States government will see fit to take action in line with Great Britain's government and I would personally favor appropriate resolutions being adopted in Congress looking toward the establishment of a Jewish National Centre in Palestine."

Wants Action by Executive and Congress.

(Signed) "SAM. J. NICHOLLS."

By Representative William F. Stevenson,
Of South Carolina.

Formation
of Jewish
State In-
evitable.

"I wish to say that it not only seems to me inevitable but wise to form a Jewish State in Palestine under the protection of the English speaking races and nations of the world with whom the French will surely co-operate. Armenia and Palestine should be put in the same category and allowed to work out their respective destinies freed from the unutterable cruelties to which they have been subjected for centuries."

(Signed)   "W. F. STEVENSON."

By Representative Charles H. Dillon,
Of South Dakota.

Approves
Declaration.

"I approve the British Declaration favoring the re-establishment of the Jewish homeland in Palestine.

Wants
Democracies
to Act.

"I favor appropriate action by the democratic governments to effect the practical consummation of the above declaration."   (Signed)   "C. H. DILLON."

By Representative Harry L. Gandy,
Of South Dakota.

Declarations
Wise and
Just.

"I am in sympathy with the Zionist movement and feel that the declarations of England, France and Italy, are wise and just.

Hopes to See
Zionism
Realized.

"I can well understand the sentiment which prompts the Jewish people to desire the re-establishment of a Jewish national home in Palestine and certainly a way ought to be open to give this to those who desire to go there."   (Signed)   "HARRY L. GANDY."

By Representative Richard W. Austin,
Of Tennessee.

Hopes for
Solution of
Jewish
Problem.

"I would be in favor of any proposition which would tend to benefit the Jewish race and I hope to find time in the near future to give Zionism the attention it merits."

(Signed)   "R. W. AUSTIN."

210

By Representative Joseph W. Byrns,
Of Tennessee.

"I am very much in sympathy with all of the aspira- Sympathizes
tions of this splendid race of people which has con- with Jewish
tributed so much to the upbuilding of our own country. Aspirations.
I regret, however, to say that I have not had the opportunity to give the question of Zionism that thorough
study and investigation to make my views either inter-
esting or valuable." (Signed) "JOSEPH W. BYRNS."

By Representative Finis J. Garrett,
Of Tennessee.

"I am not entirely clear as to the interpretations Long in
placed upon the utterances of Mr. Balfour and am not, Sympathy
therefore, prepared to give a categorical opinion. I may Zionism.
state, however, that my sympathies have been long en-
listed in behalf of the conception of the establishment
in the Holy Land of a Jewish Nation, provided, always,
this met with the desire of the Jewish people."

(Signed) "FINIS J. GARRETT."

By Representative William C. Houston,
Of Tennessee.

"I am heartily in sympathy with the effort of the Sympathizes
Jewish people to establish a National House at Pales- with
tine. In fact, I am in sympathy with the purpose in- Hopes
volved to secure action on Zionism by the Government United
of the United States as well as a Resolution in Congress States
to the same effect." Will Act.

(Signed) "W. C. HOUSTON."

By Representative Cordell Hull,
Of Tennessee.

"Jewish re-establishment in Palestine is a matter Re-establish-
which should be governed by the wishes and the welfare ment to be
of those affected or to be affected by the proposed plan. All Con-
I should be in entire harmony with such a solution of cerned.
the question." (Signed) "CORDELL HULL."

211

By Representative Lemuel P. Padgett,
Of Tennessee.

Realization
Will Benefit
Jews and
Palestine.

"I regard the movement to establish a Jewish Homeland in Palestine as a good movement for the re-organization and rehabilitation of Palestine, and also a good
movement for all Jews who may be desirous of availing
themselves of the opportunity of returning to Palestine,
and for the rehabilitation of oppressed Jews in other
countries. I should be very glad to see it succeed."

(Signed)   "L. P. PADGETT."

By Representative Eugene Black,
Of Texas.

Indorses
Balfour
Declaration.

"I regard Mr. Balfour, Secretary of State for Foreign Affairs for Great Britain, as one of the world's
great statesmen, and I have read with much interest his
statement on this question which is of such interest to
the Jewish people and their friends everywhere. I indorse it.

Restoration
Fitting and
Proper.

"My reason for approving it is that the Jewish people
have made such a large contribution to the world's store
of religion, philanthropy, and humanitarianism, that I
think that it would be fitting and proper that they should
again be restored to their ancient city—Jerusalem—and
dwell once more in the land of their fathers, that is to
say, as many of them as would care to do so.

Action is
One for
Executive.

"I think, however, that any declaration of policy
along this particular line, in so far as the United States is
concerned, should be initiated by the President, inas-
much as our Foreign affairs are largely shaped by the
Executive branch of the Government."

(Signed)   "EUGENE BLACK."

By Representative Thomas L. Blanton,
Of Texas.

In Hearty
Accord
with Dec-
larations.

"I am in hearty accord with the official Declarations
of the United States, Great Britain, France and Italy,
concerning the question of a Jewish Home Land in
Palestine."

(Signed)   "THOMAS L. BLANTON."

By Representative James P. Buchanan,
Of Texas.

"I have held a profound interest and sympathy for any competent people in obtaining an independent home and government, and this feeling for the Jews, long entertained, is more pronounced in these acute times. Therefore, I approve the indorsement by England, France and Italy, of the proposed National Home in Palestine by and for the Jewish people. Our Ideals of Self-government Must Include the Jew.

"Our American ideals are not selfish nor exclusive. They include the Jew, and especially so because of the obvious merit of the self-governing principle that has always characterized that remarkably capable race.

"I will gladly co-operate in any well considered measure to benefit the people with whom is associated such an historic past, and if that great race develops an opportune destiny by the re-occupation of its ancient heritage in the Judean country, it will please me beyond measure to witness the wonderful home-gathering in their native land. Gratified by Coming Re-establishment.

"I will approve the indorsement, by any and all of the constituted authorities of the United States, of whatever wise and independent movement is inaugurated by the Jews to attain National independence and a National Home in Palestine. Favors United States Indorsement.

"There is no doubt in my mind of the prevailing American sentiment for the successful attainment of the just and well deserved aspiration of the Jewish world to re-establish itself in the Oriental Country of its origin and historic abode." (Signed) "J. P. BUCHANAN." American Sentiment Favors Zionism.

By Representative Joe H. Eagle,
Of Texas.

"I am unalterably opposed to the Turk continuing his domination in the land of Palestine after this war. Whatever the Allies may do with Palestine after the war will have my whole support. I would like to see an independent Jewish state established there under the protection of the United States and our gallant Allies." End Turkish Domination. Establish Jewish State.

(Signed) "JOE H. EAGLE."

213

By Representative Rufus Hardy,
Of Texas.

Human Family Owes Debt to Jews.

"The Jewish people have contributed so much of benefit to the whole human family that it seems to me the whole human family owes them a great debt. To the songs of David and the book of Job happily translated into English by genius if not by inspiration, we owe a great part of the beauty and imagery and grandeur of our noble tongue. From Genesis to Malachi in the old testament as we have it, we have a heritage of poetry, of philosophy, of literature, of law, of history, and of religion which furnishes inexhaustible stores of raw material for the uses of all the ages; while the new testament has given us the lessons of undoubtedly the greatest teacher of all times. Nearly two thousand years have passed since the people who gave us all these things have been a nation without a habitation though not without a name, a people scattered over all the earth, often

Restore Their Land to the Children of Abraham.

the object of bitter hatred and persecution, enduring oppressions and hardships in almost every country and in every age until now. The land that was given as a heritage to Abraham to Isaac and to Jacob has been taken from their children and made the football of the Nations and religions and sects. For centuries it has been under the dominion of the Turk, who has proven a cruel master. Why should not the Nations give it back to the Jewish race and thus in part repay the age-old debt we owe them? I am in hearty sympathy with the suggestion of the British Government as I understand it."

(Signed)   "RUFUS HARDY."

By Representative Jeff. McLemore,
Of Texas.

Put Declarations into Effect.

"I beg to say that the proposition of a Jewish Homeland in Palestine, in accordance with the official British, French and Italian Declarations meets with my full approval, and I shall be glad to see the Declaration put into effect."

(Signed)   "JEFF. McLEMORE."

214

By Representative Joseph J. Mansfield,
Of Texas.

"I favor appropriate action by the Democratic Gov- Wants Dec-
laration Put
into Effect
ernments to effect the practical consummation of the
British Declaration approving the re-establishment of
the Jewish Homeland in Palestine."

(Signed)   "J. J. MANSFIELD."

By Representative James L. Slayden,
Of Texas.

"I have given my cordial endorsement and will un- Indorses
Declarations.
hesitatingly give my official support to the suggestion
made by Mr. Balfour, Secretary of State for Foreign
Affairs, in England, for the establishment of a National
Home for Jews in Palestine.

"President Wilson, as I understand it, is in sympathy Believes
Restoration
Just.
Pledges
Support.
with your suggestion also. I favor the declaration be-
cause I think it an act of justice to these people who
have suffered much and are entitled to a home and
country of their own. I am ready to help make the declaration on behalf of the United States Government now
or later, as the occasion may offer."

(Signed)   "JAMES L. SLAYDEN."

By Representative James C. Wilson,
Of Texas.

"I wish to say that I like the idea. I shall be glad to Will Sup-
port Plan.
support this Zionist plan personally and in every way
I can."   (Signed)   "JAMES C. WILSON."

By Representative Frank L. Greene,
Of Vermont.

Movement Welcomed by Thoughtful Men.

"A practical direction of the so-called Zionist movement that will result in the liberation of certain long pent, long stifled, energies of the Jewish race in the collective and organized expression and development of that which once made the world richer and better, must be welcomed by all thoughtful men and women.

Is More than a Political Experiment.

"If I had the idea that this propaganda had for its purpose merely another experiment in long familiar colonization schemes, that it was merely a racially clannish movement for social, economic, and political achievement to take its place among the governments of the earth as another 'nation' or 'power,' I would not write these lines. I might not be altogether out of sympathy with it on broad grounds of the common interest of humanity in the doings of other members of the family, but I would say, without hesitation, that it was no part of the business of Americans, as such, under existing circumstances.

Restoration of National Identity.

"But, I am given to understand that it has no such aim or intention. I understand that the object of this movement is to open an opportunity for some groups of the Jewish people outside of America, even in Palestine, itself, to restore their national identity in the land of their ancestors; to welcome back to those venerated scenes members of the family scattered over the face of the earth who may desire thus to repatriate themselves; and to hold out the promise of such an asylum to Jews who, with their forbears, for many centuries, have been politically (and thus socially) oppressed and homeless in certain strange lands, but whose hearts' windows have ever been opened toward Jerusalem through it all.

Will Effect Spiritual Rebirth.

"And this, I take it, not so much with the idea that there shall arise from such a reconstitution of Palestine a nation of world politicians and traffickers, as that from the return of this ancient people to their ancient seat by the side of the Cradle of Civilization, the Mediterranean, the world shall hear once more the harp of Judah, the songs of Zion, and the voices of the Hebrew prophets; and

216

sages, poets and writers, of the mighty past shall ultimately sound again in the recreation of that intellectual
sound and moral spirit that one time blessed the known
world.

"If this is some day to mean the enlargement of the
world's social and spiritual life by reinforcement of
much that was sublime in ancient Jewish culture, it is
to be welcomed." (Signed) "FRANK L. GREENE."

Will
Enhance
World's
Culture.

By Representative Edward W. Saunders,
Of Virginia.

Approves Declaration.

"I am in hearty accord with the sentiments and purposes expressed in the official declarations of England, France and Italy, on the Zionist question.

"I favor prompt action by the United States Government in line with the British Declaration.

Favors United States Action.

"I favor the adoption of an appropriate resolution by the American Congress in favor of the establishment in Palestine of a Jewish National Centre. The wonderful career of the Jewish people under the most adverse conditions, entitles them to the aid of all the civilized nations in this effort to re-establish themselves in their historic home, as a self-governing community, free to work out their own ideals and aspirations, under the protection of the Great Powers. The new conditions that will prevail in Palestine, after the expulsion of the Turk, the opportunities that will then be afforded, for the first time in centuries for the Jews to pursue life, liberty, and happiness, amid the surroundings that re-

Will freely Pursue Their Own Aspirations.

call Solomon, David, Joshua, and other great men of their race, sages, and warriors, will afford an inspiration to the Jews not only in Palestine, but in every other quarter of the world. Under the happy auspices proposed to be established, Palestine should again become a land flowing with milk and honey, and furnish a homeland for the thousands now living under the harsh conditions imposed in so many countries of the old world.

Restoration Will Prove Good Fortune for All Jews.

"The occupation of Palestine by the British forces was a happy day, not alone for the Jews in Palestine, who were thereby relieved from the oppressions of Turkish tyranny, but for every Jew wheresoever abiding, who is faithful to the traditions of his race, and recalls with pride, the achievements of his people in that land over which the great lawgiver wistfully gazed, but was forbidden to enter."   (Signed)   "E. W. SAUNDERS."

By Representative Walter A. Watson,
Of Virginia.

"I am in entire accord with the aspirations of the Jewish people to re-establish themselves in Palestine, provided it can be accomplished with due regard for the rights and immunities of the native population. I do not feel well enough acquainted with local conditions there to know when or by what means this can be best accomplished; but looking to the permanent overthrow of the dominion of the Turk in that land in the near future, I believe a suitable opportunity will be afforded through international agreement to make the experiment which the Jewish people have so much at heart and in which I take it the Gentile world sympathizes very cordially."   (Signed)   "WALTER A. WATSON." *Approves of Re-establishment in Palestine.*

By Representative C. C. Dill,
Of Washington.

"I write to congratulate you on your activity in connection with the establishment of a Jewish Homeland in Palestine. I believe such a movement is worthy of the hearty support of the American people. It may seem to many only a dream, but it is one of those dreams which should be made to come true."
(Signed)   "C. C. DILL." *Merits Support of American People.*

By Representative Lindley H. Hadley,
Of Washington.

"I know of no reason why such of the Jewish people as might desire to re-establish themselves in Palestine should not be permitted to do so, but, on the contrary, such a result appeals to me favorably."
(Signed)   "L. W. HADLEY." *Idea of Re-establishment Appeals.*

By Representative Albert Johnson,
Of Washington.

"I am glad to endorse the Zionist Movement, for which you are giving such earnest work."
(Signed)   "ALBERT JOHNSON." *Indorses Zionist Movement.*

**By Representative John F. Miller,
Of Washington.**

Jews
Natural
Guardians
of Palestine.

"The Jewish people are the natural guardians of the Holy Land, and it seems but just that at the close of this world struggle a Jewish state, based on the fundamentals of justice and democracy, should be founded there. It was in the Holy Land that the race had its genesis; it was here that the race attained its national greatness; it was from here that the race was dispersed throughout the world; so it should be here that the race again finds a dwelling place and a national home.

Jewish
Self-De-
termination
Accords
with Our
War Aims.

"We are fighting the present war for the right of self-determination, and if we throw any barrier in the way of allowing the Jewish people this right, we shall be false to the international ideal we have set up.

Favors
Formal
Recognition
by United
States.

"I trust that this country will follow the example of the great nations, associated with us in this war, and will formally recognize the right of the Jewish people to such a destiny. As a member of Congress, I will be pleased to support a resolution of this character.

Movement
Deserves
Success.

"I am pleased to make this sentiment known, and I trust that I may see this great national undertaking achieve the success it richly deserves."

(Signed)   "JOHN F. MILLER."

**By Representative John A. Moon,
Of Washington.**

Entitled
to Recog-
nition of
Nationality.

"The Jews of the world seem to desire to be recognized and localized as one great nation. The splendid part that they have performed in their duties to mankind entitle them to that distinction of nationality which they possessed before their separation. I think well of the declarations of England, France and Italy, on the Zionist question, and hope that the aspirations of the Jews may be realized, and that Palestine may become the home of all the Jews who desire to dwell therein."

(Signed)   "JOHN A. MOON."

By Representative Edward Cooper,
Of West Virginia.

"I approve strongly the declarations made by England, France and Italy, on the Zionist question, and trust the United States through Congress will at an early date adopt resolutions favoring the stand by our Allies. A fitting tribute to the valor of the Jews in our combined fight for democracy would be the establishment of a National Home in Palestine for the Jewish people. I hope "History will repeat itself" and a condition arise through the fight for liberty and justice which will return to the Jews their home.

"You can rest assured my sympathy is with your people, and I shall at all times be ready and willing to do all within my power to bring about a condition of affairs which may be desired by them."

(Signed)　"EDW. COOPER."

For Congressional Indorsement of Declarations.

Willing to Help.

By Representative Adam B. Littlepage,
Of West Virginia.

Indorses
Zionism
to Normalize
Life of Jews.

"My reasons for indorsing the Zionist movement and for favoring the British Declaration promising the establishment of a Jewish Homeland in Palestine are very simple and natural, indeed. The Jewish people have for thousands of years been an exception to the normal condition of other nations. This abnormality of the Jews consisted in being a nation without a country, a people with a language that had been practically dead, and one that had no rights of self-determination and self-government. There is no doubt that this abnormal state of the Jew had been one of the principal causes that brought about his persecution and that had aroused prejudice against him in the minds of many.

Lack of Self-
Determination
Cause of
Abnormality.

"This abnormal condition became even more acute because of the fact that the land and country that rightfully belonged to Israel had been controlled for all these centuries by a people opposed to Jews and Gentiles alike, that this language adjudged dead was the one in which the Old Testament was given to the world, and while Jews participated in every government on earth and contributed their talent and ability to all these governments, they were deprived of the opportunity to share in one of their own. There is probably no other nation on earth whose misfortunes, caused by these conditions, were so well known all over the world and, recently, as equally regretted.

Pledges
Utmost
Support.

"And now, after two thousand years of waiting and longing, out of the ruin and desolation, the Jewish people is at last to build up its ancient heritage. It will obtain its inspiration of its mighty past from the soil whence sprung its great history. Who would dare resist this noble cause, and who would shirk the support of this lofty principle? I should deem it a privilege to support this Zionist Movement to the utmost of my ability at every proper occasion."

(Signed)   "ADAM B. LITTLEPAGE."

By Representative Stuart F. Reed,
Of West Virginia.

"I feel that the Zionist movement is one of the great events of the centuries, and should enlist the interest of all Christendom." (Signed) "STUART F. REED."

Should Enlist Christian Interest.

By Representative Edward E. Browne,
Of Wisconsin.

"I fully approve of the actions of the British, French and Italian Governments, in giving their official support to the Zionist movement. The re-establishment of the Jews in their ancient homeland is desirable not only for their own welfare, but must also prove beneficial to the other Governments of the world. I am heartily in favor that our Government take similar action on this important question. I feel confident that this step will be taken by the Government of the United States sooner or later. I should, furthermore, be glad to support an appropriate resolution by Congress in favor of the establishment in Palestine of a Jewish national center.

Favors Indorsement by United States.

"I regard the effort of the Jewish people to establish a national home in Palestine as a very laudable desire, which should rightfully receive the support of all Americans. This Holy Land should go back to the Jews after being controlled by the uncivilized and barbarous Turk for so many centuries. I hope that the great holy city where Christianity had its first humble beginnings, will again be restored to the Jewish nation, its rightful owner."

Restore Holy Land to Jews— the Rightful Owners.

(Signed) "EDWARD E. BROWNE."

By Representative William J. Cary,
Of Wisconsin.

In Hearty
Accord.

"You may be assured that I am in hearty accord with the principles and underlying ideals of the British Declaration and the Zionist movement.

Believes
in Self-
determina-
tion.

"The strongest feeling of the human soul is the yearning for the land from which one and one's fathers have sprung, and this feeling has been the source of some of the noblest achievements of the human race, and as I have always been a consistent believer in the rights of all people to self-determination, I am in deep sympathy with the efforts of the Jewish Race to achieve their desire in regaining for themselves the cradle of Judaism.

Return
Palestine
to Jews.

"Believing this and realizing the great crisis that is now confronting the whole world, I am more than pleased to be quoted as being in favor of the return of Palestine to the Hebrew race."

(Signed)   "Wm. J. Cary."

By Representative David G. Classon,
Of Wisconsin.

"The declarations of England and our other allies in favor of a Jewish Homeland in Palestine has found a most responsive sentiment towards Zionism in my heart. Now that all these nations have vouched for the realization of Zionism, I can see no conceivable reason to believe that any nation which will have a voice at the peace table and in the reconstruction of the world at the close of the war, will find any ground for opposing the establishment of a Jewish state in Palestine. Everywhere the Jews have done their duty with men and money, cheerfully and fully, to the governments under which they live, as we all know in this country. The project, therefore, to help them in regaining their ancient homeland appeals strongly to the historic, just, and religious conscience of the world. A Palestinean Jewish republic would be advantageous to the Jews and to the other nations of the world. *No Ground for Opposition.*

"I know that few of the Jews of the liberal countries would go back to Palestine, but all of them in every land would realize with pride and joy that a Jewish flag floated over a state which was Jewish in language and religion and where those of their faith and nationality who desired to go there, might live in happiness and in peace. *Jews Everywhere Might Take Pride in Flag.*

"I am thus in favor of an appropriate resolution in the Congress of the United States favoring a Jewish Homeland in Palestine. I would not like to hear anyone refer any more to the Jews as the people without a country. It is my hope that they will regain their land, revive their language, and live as free and prosperous citizens of the land of Judea. Can anyone think of anything more beautiful and more just." *Favors a Congressional Resolution.*

(Signed) "DAVID G. CLASSON."

225

By Representative Henry A. Cooper,
Of Wisconsin.

In Sympathy with Zionism.

"The Principles of Zionism were first impressed upon my mind several years ago through reading a speech by Mr. Justice Brandeis. That speech was a forceful, eloquent, convincing presentation of the fundamentals of the Zionist movement, and ever since reading it the movement has had my sympathy.

Justice Demands Palestine be Restored.

"To think of the Jewish people re-established in Palestine, their ancestral home, after twenty centuries of banishment, not only stirs the imagination and awakens sympathy, but it does far more than this, for it also appeals powerfully to one's sense of justice.

Hopes United States Will Assist.

"I shall be glad to have the Government of the United States do all that it properly can do in furtherance of this essentially noble cause. This, of course, I say with the understanding that non-Jewish residents of Palestine shall forever enjoy such civil and religious liberty as is now guaranteed by our Constitution to the Jewish population in this Republic."

(Signed) "HENRY ALLEN COOPER."

By Representative John J. Esch,
Of Wisconsin.

American Indorsement Would Accord with Our War Aims.

"I heartily approve the Declarations of England, France and Italy, on the Zionist question. The carrying out of such Declarations, with the endorsement thereof by our own government, will permit the realization of the hope of the Jewish people, not only in the United States, but throughout the world. It will mean the rehabilitation of the Holy Land and relief for all time to come against Moslem tyranny and oppression. It will constitute a fitting example of what America means by self-definition of peoples based on racial lines.

Favors Resolution.

"If a resolution by Congress is necessary to this end, I favor it."

(Signed) "JOHN J. ESCH."

By Representative James A. Frear,
Of Wisconsin.

"The movement to provide a home for the Jewish people in Palestine, has brought to its support the leading men of the world, including President Wilson of our own Government, and this in itself is an effort, however tardily put forth by the civilized world, to remedy a wrong of centuries ago. *Remedy Wrong of Centuries.*

"During these days of war, when the same world is striving by force of arms to adjust differences between nations and people, it is well to note the effort on the part of the Gentiles of the twentieth century in trying to do justice to the Jewish people. *Justice to Jewish People.*

"After all these centuries, during which the world's attention has been focused upon the small country once a center of great moral and religious awakening, it now seems certain that a permanent home is to be established for those who have never lost their longing for a Jewish home in Palestine. *Permanent Jewish Home to Be Established.*

"It is one of the fruits of the world's war fought and won for the helpless and oppressed of all nations." *Among the Fruits of War.*

(Signed)   "JAMES A. FREAR."

By Representative John M. Nelson,
Of Wisconsin.

"I have not replied to your important letters, because I have nothing to say on the subject of your inquiry. This does not mean at all that I am unfriendly to the return of your people to their Homeland. *Prefers to be Silent. Presages Success.*

"I prefer to be a silent observer. I am certain, however, that Jerusalem will again be the seat of Government of the Jews."   (Signed)   "JOHN M. NELSON."

227

**By Representative Edward Voigt,
Of Wisconsin.**

Favors Restoration under Protectorate of Nations.

"I gladly give my approval to the cause of Zionism and the proposal for the restoration of the Jewish national status. I have some very good friends among the Jewish people, and know something about their aspirations in this matter. No matter what form of Government is provided in Palestine, it should be under the protectorate of all the great nations, as a result of the treaty of peace, so that there may be no harm or hatred towards any of the inhabitants of that land.

Elimination of Prejudice.

"The Jews in the land of their forefathers should be guaranteed absolutely equal rights and privileges, in trade, education, writing, speech and conscience, and they should be unhampered in their cultural and religious development. These rights and privileges should be accorded the Jews in every land. It appears to me that one of the beneficent effects of this war will be the elimination of prejudice against the Jews everywhere. I pray that as a result of the war mankind will more strongly feel that all men are brothers.

Credit to American Zionists.

"The movement to secure a proper status for the Jews in Palestine is a worthy one, and our American Jewish citizens are entitled to credit for their efforts, which mean so much for the Jews all over the world.

For Declaration by United States.

"The declarations of our Allies in favor of Zionism were very proper, and I hope that Congress or the executive branch of our government will make a like declaration."
(Signed) "EDWARD VOIGT."

**By Representative Frank W. Mondell,
Of Wyoming.**

Nations' Duty to Guarantee Jewish Independence.

"I favor the establishment of a national home for the Jewish people, and believe the nations of the earth should guarantee the independence and territorial integrity of such a Jewish state. I realize, of course, that a comparatively few of the Jewish people would ever be

Appeals to Religious Sentiment of Jew and Gentile.

permanent residents of Palestine. Nevertheless, the creation and maintenance of such a state appeals to the sense of justice and religious and moral sentiment of Jew and Gentile alike."
(Signed) "F. W. MONDELL."

228

www.ingramcontent.com/pod-product-compliance
Lightning Source LLC
Chambersburg PA
CBHW070639290526
45790CB00001B/142